Let
Your
Light
Shine

Let Your Light Shine

Bob Yandian

Whitaker House

Unless otherwise indicated, all Scripture quotations are taken from the *King James Version* (KJV) of the Bible.

Scripture quotations marked (AMP) are from the *Amplified New Testament,* ©1954, 1958, 1987, by the Lockman Foundation, and are used by permission.

LET YOUR LIGHT SHINE

Bob Yandian
Bob Yandian Ministries
P.O. Box 55236
Tulsa, OK 74155-1236

ISBN: 0-88368-360-1
Printed in the United States of America
Copyright © 1983, 1988 by Bob Yandian
Images © 1995 PhotoDisc, Inc.

Whitaker House
580 Pittsburgh Street
Springdale, PA 15144

1 2 3 4 5 6 7 8 9 10 11 12 / 05 04 03 02 01 00 99 98 97 96 95

In dedication to Loretta, my wife, whom I consider to be great in the kingdom of God. She has never failed to put me in remembrance of God's Word.

Contents

Introduction

The Sermon on the Mount is probably one of the most practical areas of teaching in the Word of God, because Jesus was instructing His disciples on how to live their lives in front of people.

I'm sure that as you were growing up, you heard a lot of things about the Beatitudes, which are the first part of the Sermon on the Mount, but you probably didn't really know what they meant. You knew they said, "Blessed are the meek," so you stood around and tried to be meek. You *heard*, but you didn't *learn*.

Before we begin our actual study of the Sermon on the Mount, let's look at some of the events that led up to Jesus taking the disciples up on the mountain and giving them the three chapters of Scripture we call the Sermon on the Mountain.

The public ministry of Jesus actually started in Matthew 4 when, at thirty years of age, He was baptized by John the Baptist, the Holy Spirit descended upon Him, and the voice of God came from heaven saying, "This is My beloved Son in whom I am well pleased." We see that He went into the wilderness to be tempted by the devil, and when He came out, He was endued with power from on high. In Acts 10:38, it says, "How God anointed Jesus of Nazareth with the Holy Ghost and power." He was anointed with the Holy Ghost when He went into the river Jordan, but He was anointed with power when He came out of the wilderness experience.

Until that time, Jesus never performed a miracle; He never healed anyone. But from then on, He started His public ministry. He gave the sermon early in His ministry.

One myth I want to explore before we get into Jesus' teaching is that the Sermon on the Mount was taught to the multitudes. It was taught *only* to the twelve disciples.

I'm sure you've seen pictures of Jesus sitting there with the multitudes around Him with a little phrase underneath it saying, "Blessed are the meek for they shall inherit the earth." He did not give the sermon to the masses; He gave it to the disciples. There are things He said on that mountain that the masses could not hear.

The multitudes followed Him, thronged Him. There were probably 60,000-100,000 people pressing in on Him. He suddenly saw that the need of the masses was so great that He separated Himself, went up into a mountain where it was difficult for the masses to follow Him, took His disciples and taught them the Sermon on the Mount. (Matt. 5:1,2.)

In chapters 5,6 and half of chapter 7, Jesus dealt with the disciples only. About halfway through chapter 7, the masses again found Jesus and the Sermon on the Mount totally changed. Jesus went back to teaching a basic salvation message.

The Sermon on the Mount is progressive. It starts with a simple teaching in Matthew 5 recognizing and isolating sin. Jesus talks about the sin of murder, then He takes up adultery, forswearing yourself, and then retaliation. In chapter 6, He leaves the area of sin and gets into good things such as giving, prayer, and fasting. He then deals with *motives*. As we progress through chapters 5 and 6, we are approaching maturity. When we get to chapter 7, He talks about one of the easiest sins to get into when you start to grow up — that is in the area of pride and judging others.

The study of the Sermon on the Mount is extremely interesting because it deals with real life. It was valid and important for Jesus' disciples then, and it is likewise valid and important for us today.

1
The Beatitudes:
Knowledge and Wisdom

The Beatitudes, which are actually the introduction to the Sermon on the Mount, serve well as a table of contents for the sermon. They are divided into two sections: taking in the Word of God and putting out the Word.

"But be ye doers of the word, and not hearers only, deceiving your own selves" (James 1:22).

Intake of the Word is what James calls being a *hearer* of the Word. *Putting out the Word* is being a *doer* of the Word. Now, we all want to be a doer of the Word, because it is in the doing that the blessings come, right? But you can't be a doer until you are a hearer. It's just like breathing. You breathe in and you breathe out; you breathe in, and you breathe out. You take in the Word, and you put out the Word.

Taking in the Word of God is called *knowledge*. The correct output or application of that knowledge is called *wisdom*. You have to have knowledge before you can produce wisdom.

Knowledge is up to you; it takes discipline to obtain it — taking the time to get into the Word and study it.

The Bible says, "Study to shew thyself approved unto God, a workman that needeth not be ashamed, rightly dividing the word of truth" (2 Tim. 2:15). But once you have taken in the Word and gained knowledge, then the Bible says, "If any of you lack wisdom, let him ask of God," (James 1:5).

Solomon, full of knowledge, asked God for the ability to produce the Word (wisdom). That is what you should be doing. You should be saying, "Lord, give me an opportunity to share. Help me put the words together." The more you study God's Word, the more the Holy Spirit will give you the right word at the right time. That is wisdom.

Isaiah 33:6 says, "And wisdom and knowledge shall be the stability of thy times, and strength of salvation." If there is anything that Christians need today, it is a stabilizer, because the devil is still knocking Christians over left and right. There are Christians who are mentally ill. Christians are becoming oppressed and depressed all around us. Being born again doesn't make you immune to the attacks of the devil; none of us are immune. But it is the Word of God that makes you stable in the midst of the attacks.

You can't stop the thoughts and doubts from coming, but those who have the Word of God in them know how to cast them down and keep their minds on the Word.

There are times I begin to look around and say, "When was the last time the devil attacked me?" Then I realize that he *has* been attacking me, I just haven't noticed it because the Word of God has been a stabilizer on the inside of me.

There are a lot of Christians today who aren't even sure they are born again. There are many people in mental institutions because they think they've committed the unpardonable sin. That is one of the big tools of the devil. The very fact that a person *wants* to get right with the Lord, but they think they can't do it is an indication that they haven't committed an unpardonable sin. But the devil has them browbeaten over it.

How can a person get strength of salvation?

Through knowing the Word of God and applying it — knowledge and wisdom. When you apply the Word in your life, you have strength of salvation. There's no devil that can convince you that you're not saved. You know you are. Feelings have nothing to do with it.

Taking in the Word —

Wisdom and knowledge put together are going to explain the Beatitudes. We're going to start out with intake of the Word of God, or knowledge. So let's begin in Matthew, chapter 5.

MATTHEW 5:3

Blessed are the poor in spirit: for theirs is the kingdom of heaven.

The Greek word for "blessed" is *makarios* which means "happy, jubilant." The word "poor" here actually means "to be destitute," or "bankrupt."

How could someone who is bankrupt be happy in spirit? It goes on to explain how: "For theirs is the kingdom of heaven."

This is the Beatitude of the new birth, and it is telling us that Jesus died for the ungodly; salvation is provided for the sinner. (1 Tim. 1:15.) Jesus didn't die just for the elect, or just for the few who would accept Him; He died for the whole world. (2 Cor. 5:19; 1 John 2:2.)

Did you ever think about making witnessing good news? Go up to a sinner and say, "Glory, are you blessed!"

"I'm what?" he would probably respond.

"You're blessed."

"I am? Why?"

"The kingdom of heaven belongs to you."

"It does?"

For years we've been saying, "You wretched sinner. Give up your cussing, your smoking and your chewing; and

13

maybe God might give you some grace and find a place for you in His kingdom. But first you have to clean yourself up." No. Their sins have already been put away. The only thing that's holding them away from the riches of heaven is their attitude toward the Lord Jesus Christ. All they need to do is accept Him.

If you haven't accepted the kingdom of heaven and the blessings of God, that's not God's fault, it's your fault. He has already blessed you. If you're sick today, you're still blessed. Why? Because healing already belongs to you. If you're broke today, you're blessed anyway because prosperity belongs to you. The riches of heaven already belong to you whether you've accepted them or not.

VERSE 4

Blessed are they that mourn: for they shall be comforted.

Now when you mourn, you have the Comforter, the Holy Spirit. (John 14:16.) The new birth does not stop trials, it brings us comfort and answers *in the midst of them.* The new birth of verse 3 brings us the Comforter of verse 4.

When you used to mourn, there was no comforter in your life. Your friends were in the same shape you were and could offer no *real* comfort. The Holy Spirit, your Comforter, will be with you now forever.

Now look at the next verse.

VERSE 5
Blessed are the meek for they shall inherit the earth.

"Meek" is a word that has been grossly misused. People often think to be meek is to be "weak." When we picture a meek person, we always think of a scrawny guy who lets everyone run over him. He's easy to pick on, therefore he's meek. No. The word "meek" does not mean to be weak; it means "to be teachable."

14

If you are meek, you are teachable. James tells us to "receive with *meekness* the engrafted Word," (James 1:21). That means "be teachable while the Word is being taught." There are a lot of things you can learn if you'll just be teachable. I have learned more from people with whom I disagree than from people with whom I agree. I've been to services many times when some man will get up and preach what sounds like a lot of unbelief. Instead of closing him off, I remain teachable and start looking for things with which I can agree. I might find only one or two points, but there have been times when I've remembered those points and was able to use them somewhere. I probably disregarded 98 percent of his message, but the 2 percent I remembered was usable. I stayed teachable.

What happens if you stay teachable? You inherit the earth.

The Greek word translated "earth" here is *ge;* it literally means "land." I'm teachable now; does that mean I can inherit the land now? Yes. This verse is teaching prosperity. When you are teachable in the Word of God, the land comes to you. "The wealth of the sinner is laid up for the just" (Prov. 13:22).

One of the first things you need to do in the Christian life, therefore, is become teachable. Read good books. Get under a pastor you can trust and start learning the Word of God. And God will start giving you prosperity.

When I was growing up, I was one of the most unteachable people you ever saw. If anyone ever mentioned they had money, I stood back and thought they were carnal. I thought that you couldn't be spiritual and have money. I thought poverty was next to godliness; but it's not.

One day I was listening to someone teach about prosperity and I was thinking. *I'm not sure about that.* Then it hit me: *He's teaching right from the Word. Who am I to argue with it?* So I started looking at the Word for myself and I put away that hard attitude. I became teachable, and I started getting prosperous.

There is something else this verse indicates: If we're going progressively through the Sermon on the Mount, then prosperity must come early in the Christian life because it's at the first of the sermon. The Lord wants you to have riches early so that you can give into the kingdom.

Look where we are going. In verse 4 we got comforted and in verse 5 we started getting prosperous. That's not bad, is it? After you get prosperity, notice what the next verse says.

VERSE 6
Blessed are they which do hunger and thirst after righteousness; for they shall be filled.

Meekness, which is opening yourself up to the Word and becoming teachable, produces a hunger and thirst for more. "Hunger and thirst" is one of the most beautiful terms used to describe taking in the Word of God because it compares it to a natural hunger and thirst. "Man shall not live by bread alone, but by every word that proceedeth out of the mouth of God," (Matt. 4:4) meaning that you are a two-fold being: a natural person but also a spiritual person. Just as the natural man feeds on natural food, the spiritual man must feed on spiritual food, which is the Word of God.

When a baby is born in this earth, he first becomes teachable or opens himself up to take in food by drinking milk. That milk causes the body to start growing and produces an appetite in that baby for more food. He then goes from drinking milk to eating more complicated food like meat and vegetables because the needs of the body become more complicated. The body begins to grow and its capacity for food begins to grow.

It is the same way in the Christian life — you start off with the milk of the Word and then the milk produces a hunger and thirst in you for more complicated food, or for deeper doctrines of the Word of God.

Hunger and thirst can only be satisfied *temporarily*. They always return. You can't live on yesterday's meal; you can't live on last week's meal. You need to eat every day. It's the same way in the spirit realm; you can't live on yesterday's blessings or last Sunday's sermon. You need to take in the Word of God *daily*.

I want you to notice something else in this verse. It says that those who hunger and thirst "shall be filled." This indicates that God never gives you a snack; He always serves you a feast. Even when you come to Him with only the slightest twinge of hunger, He throws out a banqueting table. He always fills you.

In the natural, in your human body, moderation is good. But in the spirit realm, it's all right to be a glutton. This whole attitude is brought out in Ephesians 5:18 which says, "And be not drunk with wine, wherein is excess; but be *filled* with the spirit." When you hunger and thirst, God wants to fill you so much that it's coming out your ears! When you think you've studied the Word enough, study more. When you think you've prayed enough, pray longer. In other words, have some dessert, too! In the spirit realm it's all right.

Titus 2:11,12 says, "For the grace of God that bringeth salvation hath appeared unto all men, teaching us that denying ungodliness and worldly lusts, we should live soberly, righteously, and godly, in this present world." In the natural, everything should be in moderation.

Putting Out the Word —

We've taken in the Word in verses 3-6, and by the time we get to verse 7, we've gotten filled. What happens when you get filled? It starts to spill over, and you can give it out. That verse tells us what to do then.

VERSE 7

Blessed are the merciful: for they shall obtain mercy.

Mercy is grace in action. *Mercy* is treating others as the Lord treats you. When you begin to hunger and thirst after righteousness, and you begin to take in the Word of God, you begin to find out that God has treated you in *grace*. He gives out of a loving heart. You got born again by grace; you got filled with the Holy Spirit by grace; and you get healed by grace. No one ever worked for, earned, or deserved his salvation or his healing. You just took it by faith.

When you begin to understand the heart of God, then you can go out and start treating others the way He treats you. Even if they don't like you, you still give to them. Even if they don't love you, you still love them.

You start pouring out mercy, and guess what you're going to reap? Mercy. This verse is teaching the law of sowing and reaping. You get back what you sow.

It also brings out another point — you always reap *more* than you sow. If you want love, sow love. But you better get ready because you're going to get back more love than you sowed. If you sowed finances, you'll get back finances "good measure, pressed down, and shaken together, and running over" (Luke 6:38).

That is how the Lord provides; and how He is saying it will work the same way with you. As you sow mercy and love in other people's lives, you'll reap it.

VERSE 8

Blessed are the pure in heart: for they shall see God.

"Pure in heart" is not referring to the new birth that was covered in verse 3. It is referring to those who walk in forgiveness. When you start sowing mercy, not everyone is going to appreciate it and thank you. Some people are going to revile you. There's a tendency at that point for you to get out of fellowship with the Lord and start reviling back, getting mad, and harboring unforgiveness.

Jesus tells us to remain pure in heart. How do we do that?

First John 1:9 says, "If we confess our sins, he is faithful and just to forgive us our sins, and to cleanse us from all unrighteousness." That is how we remain pure in heart.

You ask, "Yes, but is this verse saying that if we don't remain pure in heart, we won't see God?"

That's right.

Look at the word "see." In the Greek language there is more than one word for *see.* One word means "seeing with the natural eye," such as in the sentence: I *see* that piece of chalk. But there is another word for seeing which has to do with revelation knowledge. Have you ever been sitting in a meeting and the minister was teaching the Word and you said, "Yes, I *see* "? You didn't mean that you saw with your natural eye; you meant that you got revelation on it. That is the word used in this verse. The word means "to perceive."

You'll never *perceive* God or know His character unless you remain pure in heart because if you don't remain pure in heart nothing will work.

Psalm 66:18 says, "If I regard iniquity in my heart, the Lord will not hear me." Your prayers won't work. Your faith won't work if you have unforgiveness because the Word says, "When ye stand praying, forgive," (Mark 11:25). We know that communion won't work if you don't examine yourself before you partake of it. "For this cause many are weak and sickly among you, and many sleep" (1 Cor. 11:30).

So what should we do? Examine ourselves and remain pure in heart. When we remain pure in heart our giving will work, our prayers will work, communion will work, we'll walk in health, and we'll begin to perceive more and more the true character of the lord.

VERSE 9
Blessed are the peacemakers: for they shall be called the children of God.

Peacemakers are witnesses. Ephesians 6 says that we are to wear our helmet of salvation, our breastplate of righteousness, our sword of the spirit, and our feet are to be shod with the preparation of the gospel of *peace*. Peace is referring to witnessing, and your feet are what take you to witness. Isaiah 52:7 says, "How beautiful upon the mountains are the feet of him that bringeth good tidings, that publisheth *peace*."

Peacemaking is the doctrine of reconciliation. Look at 2 Corinthians 5:19. "To wit, that God was in Christ, reconciling the world unto himself, not imputing their trespasses unto them; and hath committed unto us the word of reconciliation." Reconciliation means that God has already made peace. The first thing the angels said when Jesus was born was, ". . . on earth peace, good will toward men" (Luke 2:14). Jesus said, "Peace I leave with you, my peace I give unto you" (John 14:27). That is the good news of the gospel. Be a peacemaker. Walk up to a sinner and say, "God's already made peace with you. He did it through the cross. God's not mad at you." That is the ministry of peace.

Notice what the next part of verse 9 says, "For they shall be called the children of God." Witnessing doesn't *make* you a child of God; it lets it be known that you *are* a child of God.

Another important thing you need to see is that Jesus doesn't even talk about witnessing until this verse, which is the next to the last verse of the Beatitudes. That indicates that witnessing does not come until later in the Christian life. In most churches, the moment a person is born again, he is thrust out to start witnessing. That is a tragic mistake.

New believers are in no position to witness because they haven't taken in enough of the Word to be able to put it out effectively.

There is a church in California which has what I consider a good program. When people get born again there, they are required to go through a new converts course. They are separated from the congregation and taught the basics on righteousness, on justification, on the new birth, on being filled with the Spirit, on judgements, and all the things that we know and take for granted. Then they are brought out into the congregation where they can begin to take in the meat of the Word. In other words, they are put in a spiritual nursery where they are fed with milk until they are able to handle the meat, and then they are put out where the meat is served.

Many celebrities have been born again in that church, and the pastor refuses to let them speak or do anything in the church until they've been in there for a year and have taken in the Word. That's very good. I heartily commend the man. So often, we get someone off the street who has a great testimony and we make him a Sunday school superintendent. He doesn't know any Word and he is trying to instruct people, half of whom know more than he does.

Babies do not produce babies, adults produce babies. That's true in the natural and that's true in the spiritual. The moment people are born again, they should be told to sit down and learn God's Word. (Matt. 11:28,29.)

VERSES 10-12
Blessed are they which are persecuted for righteousness' sake: for theirs is the kingdom of heaven.

Blessed are ye, when men shall revile you, and persecute you, and shall say all manner of evil against you falsely, for my sake.

Rejoice, and be exceeding glad: for great is your reward in heaven: for so persecuted they the prophets which were before you.

These verses are the Beatitudes of maturity. He indicates that maturity is marked by your ability to rejoice despite the circumstances. Rejoicing in persecution is not being moved by the circumstances around you; it's being moved only by the Word in you.

The words, "for righteousness' sake" are probably the three most important words in that verse. You are not blessed when you are persecuted for just any reason, but you are blessed when you are persecuted for righteousness' sake.

We have gone from the Beatitude of the new birth to the Beatitude of maturity — first taking in the Word and then putting it out.

2
Let Your Light Shine

As we move into the next part of the Sermon on the Mount, we see two more qualities of the believer: salt and light. This introduces a theme which will run through the remainder of the sermon. As salt, we should retain our savor, and as light, we should make sure we shine forth on all men. Salt and light are two common elements we cannot live without.

Relationship and Fellowship —

When a person gets born again, he actually moves into *two* areas with the Lord Jesus Christ: He has a relationship with Him, which is *eternal* and he is in fellowship with Him, which is *temporal*. These two areas have been overlooked for years, and very few people see a difference in them. Few teachers ever teach on them, and few churches ever mention them. Most churches just teach that when you get born again, you become a Christian, and then you're kind of left on your own. If you sin, you're going to hell. If you don't sin, you're going to heaven. So, the whole Christian life is a series of trying and trying to live a good life.

These are things that are yours eternally and are included in your relationship with Jesus. They were given to you the moment you were born again. Eternal life was imparted to you. You became an eternal priest. You were given righteousness, and even when you sin and miss it, God still sees you as righteous, because He sees you in Christ.

You always have a relationship with the Lord, but you can break your fellowship with Him. At any moment, you are either *in* fellowship with the Lord, or you are *out* of fellowship with the Lord. When you are in fellowship, you are called spiritual, and when you are out of fellowship, you are called carnal.

When you commit a sin, it separates you from fellowship; it does not separate you from your relationship.

Let me demonstrate the difference. My son, Robbie, came home after school, and my wife was in the kitchen making dinner. She said, "Dinner is going to be ready in just a little while, so don't get into the cookie jar."

He said, "All right Mommie, I won't."

She went into the bedroom and was folding clothes when she heard, *tinkle, tinkle, clink, clink*. She went into the kitchen, and there was Robbie up on the counter with his hand in the jar. She said, "I told you not to get into that cookie jar; go to your room right now and sit on your bed until dinner is ready."

He whimpered and ran up the stairs and into his room and closed the door.

A little while later, we all sat down at the dinner table, and he came down to eat. You can probably remember what it was like — the silence. You could cut it with a knife. No one said anything.

We're not talking about relationship here. He's my son. Him getting a cookie out of the cookie jar did not nullify the fact that he's still my son. What was broken was our fellowship. And when fellowship is gone, communication is gone. That's what happens when you sin: You sever your fellowship with the Lord and lose your ability to communicate with Him. Again, Psalm 66:18 says, "If I regard iniquity in my heart, the Lord will not hear me." That's regarding iniquity in your heart, knowing you are out of fellowship, but being too full of pride to admit it.

So, Robbie sat there and everyone was waiting for two words: "I'm sorry." When he said them, they cleared the air, and we all hugged each other. We told him that everything was all right now but, "Just don't do it again." And everything was back to normal.

The way to get back into fellowship, when you are out of fellowship with the Lord is 1 John 1:9. "If we confess our sins, he is faithful and just to forgive us our sins, and to cleanse us from all unrighteousness." That scripture is not written to sinners; it is written to believers. First John 1:9 is a big "I'm sorry" to the Lord. It clears the air and gets us back in fellowship with Him. The sin didn't sever our relationship, it severed our fellowship.

The important thing in the Christian life is to stay in fellowship and grow in the Word. That's the only way you're going to be any benefit to yourself, and to other people, and to God.

When you're out of fellowship with the Lord, you feel miserable, and the longer you stay there, the more miserable you get, because you're usually full of pride. You know you did something wrong, but you don't want to admit it. The most miserable people on the face of the earth today are not sinners; they are Christians who are out of fellowship with the Lord. I've been around some sinners who were fun to be around. They were happy-go-lucky. They knew they were going to hell, but they were going to have a good time on the way.

I used to manage a retail store, which when I took it over had some employees who were sinners and some who were saints. I made a policy, from that point on, to hire all Christians. I should have gone one step further and made sure that they were in fellowship with the Lord and were walking in line with His Word.

I had some Christians working at the store who were miserable to be around. They were never happy, they were always gloomy and down. I had sinners who worked there who I would witness to, who were happy-go-lucky, yet they were on their way to hell.

One of the sinners asked me about one of the Christians. He said, "What's wrong with that guy over there? He's always unhappy; he's always miserable." I hated to tell him, "It's because he's a Christian." It's difficult to get specific and say, "That guy is born again all right, but he's out of fellowship with God; and he's miserable because his spirit is smiting him over everything he's doing. His own life is miserable, and he just spreads misery, too."

On the other hand, the best people in the world are faith people, who are in fellowship with God and are filled with His Word. Everything they speak is the Word, and the joy of the Lord is inside of them. His Word produces joy, His Word produces strength. His Word produces stability in life. That's the kind of person that unbelievers are going to come to and say, "What have you got? I want what you've got."

You Are Salt —

Matthew 5:13

> Ye are the salt of the earth: but if the salt have lost his savour, wherewith shall it be salted? it is thenceforth good for nothing, but to be cast out, and to be trodden under foot of men.

Salt is a preservative. It keeps things from spoiling. Before we had refrigeration, we used salt to preserve food. Jesus is teaching here that we are salt, we preserve things around us. The most interesting thing is that we are the salt of the *land* (*ge*; see v. 5). You live right now in the United States of America, a plot of ground. What is it that has made the United States of America the best country in the world?

Someone might say, "It's because of our great legislation." With some of the legislation we've had, we should have gone down the tubes years ago. No, it is the salt that's here.

We can hold our hands up and say, "It's because of us. We're the salt of this earth. We're the ones that keep our nation from spoiling. We're the ones holding back the flood tides of the devil who would love to destroy this land right now." We preserve this land and we keep it functioning.

But salt can lose its savor. And as the salt, you can lose your savor by getting out of fellowship with the Lord. You see, salt is not for itself. Salt is to be put on other things to preserve them. Your life is not for yourself. The reason you got born again, Spirit-filled, and started walking in faith, is so that your life could become a blessing to others. But, when you get out of fellowship with the Lord, and you remain out of fellowship, you become stagnant and stale, and the salt loses its ability to season.

"It is thenceforth good for nothing, but to be cast out, and to be trodden under foot of men." Immediately, the first thing people think is, *See there, if you get out of fellowship with God, He's going to cast you into hell.* This is not what this says, because you're not going to be trodden under men's feet in hell. This verse is saying that in this lifetime, you're not going to be good for anything except to be a doormat for the rest of the world to walk on.

Did you know there are believers today who are being run roughshod over by the world, and they don't even realize that "greater is he that is in you, than he that is in the world" (1 John 4:4)? They don't have any revelation of that. Why? Because although they are born again, and they may even be Spirit-filled, they are out of fellowship with God. They've lost their ability to season everything around them, and all they are good for is to be stepped on by other men.

If you stay in fellowship with the Lord, if you do keep your savor, circumstances of life won't run over you; you'll dictate to them. When circumstances go wrong, a person who knows who he is in Christ Jesus will grab those circumstances and say, "In the name of Jesus, you will work out to my good." And, he will turn them around. That is a person who becomes effective in life and knows the salt that's in him.

Keep Your Savor —

You keep the savor in the salt by having salt *in yourself*. (Mark 9:50.) Salt is a type of the Word of God. Remember that you cannot put salt out until first you have salt in yourself. You cannot season the land around you and season lives around you until you are full of salt yourself.

Look at Colossians 4:5,6. "Walk in wisdom toward them that are without, redeeming the time. Let your speech be always with grace, seasoned with *salt*, that ye may know how you ought to answer every man." Before you can walk in wisdom, you have to have knowledge, or take in the Word. Speech is wisdom in action. You are putting out the Word of God with your speech.

How is your word seasoned with salt?

You have a salt shaker on the inside of you and you just sprinkle salt over every word that comes out of your mouth. But, the salt shaker must stay full; therefore, you must keep taking salt (the Word) in so that you'll have salt in you to sprinkle on the words that you put out.

Look at Job 6:6. "Can that which is unsavoury be eaten without salt? or is there any taste in the white of an egg?" Probably one of the most bland things you'll ever eat is the white of an egg; it needs salt.

The "white of an egg" here is referring to things in your life which are unsavory. There are certain foods that have flavor and a lot of foods that have no flavor so they require salt. It's just like that in the things of life. There are certain things that you do enjoy doing, but there are also things that you don't enjoy. There is no flavor in them.

For example, I had a job one summer working on an assembly line. I pounded rubber stoppers into holes and screwed nuts on bolts for eight hours a day. I was bored. I continually looked forward to lunch hour, breaks, and getting off of work. After awhile, I began to realize that I had a salt shaker on the inside of me, and that when things were untasty and things were bland, I could shake salt on them. I could put the Word on them. The Word made that which was unsavory, suddenly savory.

The people around me would be complaining and gripping about their jobs, and I'd just be saying, "Glory to God, hallelujah," and screwing nuts on bolts. I would praise Jesus, quote His Word, meditate on the Word and get edified on the inside. The people around me thought I was bonkers. But I had salt in me, and I could salt the things around me.

Jesus didn't say, *"Try* to be salt." He said, "You are *salt.*"

There is nothing more obnoxious than a Christian *trying* to witness or a person trying to force the Lord on someone. Yet, there is nothing more beautiful than people who can't help but talk about the Lord. They are so full of the Word that every word that comes out is full of salt. People around them aren't turned off by that, they are very much attracted to it.

It's not always *saying something* that is important. It's just *being* a witness. (Acts 1:8) The Bible says, "Whatsoever you do in word or deed, do all in the name of the Lord Jesus" (Col. 3:17). Don't try to be salt, just be what you are.

That is what happened to me when I worked as a package boy at a grocery store, while I was in high school. I was raised in a Christian home, and in our home we didn't criticize people. Even when they did things wrong, we looked at them in the light of the Word of God.

One day a lady came through the checkout line at the store who did several things that really irritated me. She made me undo boxes and bags and put things back the way she wanted them. She scrutinized everything I did. The line piled up, and I got frustrated because the store was jammed that day. Everything she did just ticked me off. When I took her groceries to her car and came back in, I verbally let her have it. I just criticized her up one side and down the other.

The manager's wife came over to me and said, "That's strange; that's the first time I've *ever* heard you run anybody down."

I had never stopped to think about it. I hadn't *tried* not to criticize people; it was just so ingrained in me not to do it that when I *did* criticize someone, it sounded strange.

Light of the World —

VERSE 14

Ye are the light of the world. A city that is set on an hill cannot be hid.

The Greek word for "world" in this verse is *kosmos* meaning "the world system." We couldn't use the word *land* (*ge*) here because we aren't the light of the land. The sun is the light of the land. When the sun comes up, it lights the physical land. But the analogy goes further. We don't just live on a physical piece of property; we also live in a world system. The world system is backed by the prince of darkness who is the devil. In that darkness, we are a light. It is impossible for darkness to overcome light. Light has all the power. Darkness is the absence of light; therefore, when light comes in, the absence cannot overtake the presence.

VERSE 15

Neither do men light a candle, and put it under a bushel, but on a candlestick; and it giveth light unto all that are in the house.

"Candle" here refers to an oil lamp and "bushel" refers to a clay pot that holds a bushel. "Neither do men light a *lamp* and put it under a *clay pot that holds a bushel*."

Do you remember in the Old Testament when Gideon's army took clay pots and put them over their lamps? They were all standing on a hill and no one could see them. At the last minute, the men all shattered their clay pots and the light began to shine forth.

You can be on a hill, and you can have the light, but if you put the light under a clay pot, no one can see it. If your clay pot is over your lamp, you are not in fellowship with the Lord. Shatter that pot with 1 John 1:9.

Notice, He tells you to "Put your lamp on a lampstand." In the ancient world, lampstands were put up near the ceiling because the higher the light was placed, the more light it gave all around the house.

Let your light shine out to the world. Put your lamp on the lampstand and your city on the hill where they will do the most good — where the most people will see your light.

When your city is in the valley or your lamp is under the clay pot, you are *out of fellowship* with the Lord. When your city is on the hill and your lamp is on the lampstand, you are *in fellowship* with Him. Keep your lamp on the lampstand and your city on the hill.

He first tells you to let your light shine to the *world* and then He says to let your light shine in the *house*. Don't just be a witness to the world; also be a witness in your home. Keep your home in order.

VERSE 16

Let your light so shine before men, that they may
see your good works, and glorify your Father which
is in heaven.

Don't *make* it shine, *let* it shine. If you make it shine,
you take the glory. If you'll let God work through you, He'll
get all the glory.

3
Fulfilling the Law

MATTHEW 5:17

Think not that I am come to destroy the law, or the prophets: I am not come to destroy but to fulfill.

This verse introduces the theme of Matthew 5. Jesus came to fulfill the law. He didn't come to put it away as the disciples often thought that He did, but to keep it.

The first things the disciples probably thought of when Jesus said "the law" were such things as "Jesus won't worship idols," or "He will honor His mother. He won't commit adultery. He won't steal anything or murder anyone." It is just the same with people today: When you mention sin, they think about outward sins. When you say murder, they think about pulling out a knife or a gun and killing someone.

Inward Sins —

VERSE 18
For verily I say unto you, Till heaven and earth pass, one jot or one tittle shall in no wise pass from the law, till all be fulfilled.

Jots and *tittles* are the smallest letters and marks in the Hebrew alphabet. They are things that are easily overlooked.

What if I said, "In the Sermon on the Mount, we're not going to leave out one word. We're going to dot every *i*, we're going to cross every *t*." That expression means we're not going to overlook any little part. Jesus was saying the same thing about the law.

I'm sure the disciples were thinking, *Yes, okay. We understand.* But when He started explaining, their eyes started to get big; because Jesus not only mentioned things they associated with outward sins, He brought out the roots of sin. When He mentioned adultery, they automatically thought of the outward act. Jesus explained where adultery begins — with the *thoughts.* That's what Jesus was referring to when He said, "jots and tittles."

We always think of something outward when we think about sin, but look at what God says are the seven sins He hates. (Prov. 6:16-19.) "These six things doth the Lord hate: yea, seven are an abomination unto him." The first one is "a proud look." The Bible says "pride goeth before destruction" (Prov. 16:18). The next one is "a lying tongue." There are many people today who don't know their tongue controls their entire body. They don't even think about what their tongue is doing. They make sure their hands and feet and the other outward parts of their body are doing what's right, but they never think about their tongue. Do you know what the tongue is dominated by? The mind — the inward man. You form thoughts in your mind, and they express themselves through your tongue.

The third sin is "hands that shed innocent blood." This is murder. It is the only outward sin mentioned. Out of seven sins, we only have one outward sin and the other six are sins of the thoughts or sins of the tongue.

The other four sins are "an heart that deviseth wicked imaginations, feet that be swift in running to mischief, a false witness that speaketh lies; and he that soweth discord among the brethren."

God is majoring on what we would consider jots and tittles. He's pointing out the seven things He hates, and they are the ones we would brush out of the way while we go around looking for the big letters of the law.

Whosoever therefore shall break one of these least commandments, and shall teach men so, he shall be called least in the kingdom of heaven: but whosoever shall do and teach them, the same shall be called great in the kingdom of heaven.

For I say unto you, that except your righteousness shall exceed the righteousness of the scribes and Pharisees, ye shall in no case enter into the kingdom of heaven.

The least commandments are the jots and tittles, and Jesus points out they are *major* points of the law. Jesus told the disciples, "If you keep them and teach men to keep them, I'm going to call you great in the kingdom of heaven; your righteousness will exceed the righteousness of the scribes and Pharisees."

What is the righteousness of the scribes and Pharisees?

They were considered great men. They went to the temple seven times a day, they prayed long prayers three times a day, for as much as an hour or two each. They gave large sums of money and they fasted a lot. These men were great men when it came to being *outwardly* spiritual or *outwardly* righteous. But they were big on not keeping the jots and tittles of the law. They did not watch the *inward* sins: They were full of proud looks, full of deceitfulness; swift in running to mischief; and they sowed discord among the brethren.

I'm sure the disciples were surprised, because if there was anyone who looked righteous, it was the scribes and Pharisees. But Jesus said their righteousness was all outward.

Jesus is going to tell the disciples how to recognize sin: You don't wait to recognize it until it shows up on the outside; you catch it while it is still on the inside. If you can stop the thought, the deed will never take place.

Thou Shalt Not Murder —

VERSE 21
Ye have heard that it was said by them of old time, Thou shalt not kill; and whosoever shall kill shall be in danger of the judgment.

Jesus is quoting from Exodus 20:13 — the sixth commandment. But turn to Matthew 19:18. Jesus, when asked by the rich young ruler which of the commandments he needed to keep, said, "Thou shalt do no *murder* . . . ." Do no what? *Murder* is the word Jesus used here.

Is there a difference between killing and murder?

There definitely is. Matthew 19:18 is the *only* time in the King James Version that that word is *correctly translated*. The word is *murder;* it is not kill. The Bible does not contradict itself. In fact, if you have another translation of the Bible which is closer to the original, look at Exodus 20:13 and you'll see that the commandment does not say, "Thou shall not kill." It says, "Thou shall not murder."

The Bible says there is a time to kill, and there is a time to heal (Eccl. 3:3), but there never is a time to murder.

Killing Condoned —

The Bible is explicit: There is a time to kill. Capital punishment is condoned in the Word of God. Genesis 9:6 says, "Whoso sheddeth man's blood, by man shall his blood be shed." Throughout the Law, there were capital crimes for which people were stoned.

"Yea, but that was the Old Testament," someone might say.

Let's look at what the New Testament says about capital punishment. Romans 13 is dealing with the government and the law of the land. It says in verse 1, "The powers that be are ordained of God." That's talking about government. It goes on to say we are to obey them and their laws "for he beareth not the *sword* in vain." That's referring to capital punishment. (v. 4.)

Killing in the time of war is also condoned in the Word of God. There is no such thing in the Word of God as a conscientious objector. God not only commends going to war and defending your country, He commands it.

Yes, but the Bible says, "Thou shalt not kill," people say.

No, it doesn't. It says, "Thou shalt not murder." Remember in Proverbs 6:16, the only outward sin that was spoken against was "hands that shed *innocent* blood."

What kind of blood? Innocent blood. That's murder. So if you turn that around you'll have it: It is all right, at times, when hands shed *guilty* blood.

When the children of Israel went into the land of Canaan, there were times when God told them to pull out the sword and to kill all the inhabitants. The book of Joshua is a very bloody book, but God blessed His people throughout the whole book.

Someone might ask, "How could God bless the children of Israel when they were killing innocent people?"

They did not kill *innocent* people. The Bible talks about the iniquity of the Amorites. God gave them years and years to repent of their evil deeds. God's grace is long suffering. Finally their wickedness had become so bad that by the time the children of Israel came in they had developed into mad dogs. Just like a mad dog that is frothing at the mouth, the only thing that could be done for the good of everyone else was to get rid of them. And that's what God had to do. When the Israelites went in He said, "I can't bless you until you get rid of them." So the Israelites slaughtered them all and God condoned it.

Murder of the Mind —

When Jesus mentioned murder, the first thing the disciples probably thought about was the sword. The first thing we might think about would be a gun. But Jesus goes back to the source of the sin and explains what murder really is.

VERSE 22
But I say unto you that whosoever is angry with his brother without a cause shall be in danger of the judgment, and whosoever shall say to his brother, Raca, shall be in danger of the council: but whosoever shall say, Thou fool, shall be in danger of hell fire.

The same judgement seat is going to judge thoughts in the same way it judges deeds.

Notice the word "angry." "Whosoever is angry with his brother." The Greek translation of that says, "Whosoever is *lightly angry* with his brother." Jesus brings out here exactly what was brought out in Proverbs 6 — that the worst sins are sins of thought, such as anger. Proverbs 6:18 says the Lord hates "a heart that deviseth wicked imaginations." Here we see that murder starts on the inside with a thought.

The devil cannot grab your hand and make you get a gun and shoot someone. You've heard people say, "I just don't know what came over me; I just pulled a gun and shot." They might have been demon-possessed, that's true. But they had to open up the door for that demon possession a long time before. No demon just jumps on someone and possesses them. He works on their thoughts and will, first. He gets them into confusion and doubt, and then he

38

gets them into fear. Fear is the doorway through which the demon comes in.

In the case of murder, let's suppose the person wasn't demon-possessed, he was only influenced by Satan. How did it start? It started with light anger. Someone did something that offended him. Instead of dismissing that thought and putting it away, he started harboring it. He then acted on the thought and committed the murder. Light anger begins to fester; when it festers, it turns into harder anger. It turns into outbursts of emotion. It then begins to form into words; then, the deed manifests.

You can't stop the thoughts from *coming*, but you don't have to *accept* them and *meditate* on them. If you stop thinking the thought, you can stop the deed. The deed would have never come along if you would have nipped the thought in the bud, because what's on the inside will eventually come out if you don't get rid of it. (Prov. 23:7)

Jesus is not saying here that the thought is as bad as the deed. He's saying that the thought *is* the deed. The moment you thought it and meditated on it, God saw you pull out the sword and murder the person.

Judging Others Spiritually —

VERSE 22
And whosoever shall say to his brother, Raca, shall be in danger of the council.

You're probably thinking, *That doesn't apply to me, I've never said "Raca" in my whole life.* I've never said Raca either but let's go on a little further in the verse. "But whosoever shall say, Thou fool, shall be in danger of hell fire." We've said "fool" before, haven't we?

To understand what Jesus is saying, we're going to have to look back at the time when it was written and the customs of that day.

When light anger begins to fester, if you do not take care of it, it turns into more explosive anger. And it's going to come out of your mouth in one of two ways. It's going to come out either as "Raca" or "Thou fool." "Raca" and "Thou fool" stand for two different things.

First of all, you are not a citizen of only one world, you are a citizen of two worlds. You live in the natural human world, but you're also a spirit creature and are in God's world. You are really walking before two audiences — God and man. You must first walk circumspectly before God. But you also have to walk before men. There are certain things you can say that offend God; there are other things you can say that offend men. If you say things that offend God, you're going to face His judgement. If you say things that offend men, you'll have to face man's council. Man's council here is governments, judges, juries, and court systems. The Greek word for *council* is *Sanhedrin*. The Sanhedrin was the council of that day; it was the jury or the legal court. "Whosoever shall say to his brother, Raca, shall be in danger of facing the Sanhedrin."

What does *Raca* mean? *Raca* stands for words that offend men. I'm sure that when Jesus said "Raca" the disciples' ears turned red. It's just like someone getting mad and calling you a s.o.b. Now you can see what the disciples felt when Jesus said "Raca."

You say, "Yes, but Christians wouldn't say things like that." They *do*. In fact, there are probably things that would come out of your mouth that would surprise you, if you allowed light anger to get in. The devil keeps that anger coming up and coming up, until eventually, something comes out of your mouth that you can't believe you said. And the moment it does, there will be people in the world waiting to grab you and haul you to court because you just don't stand before God in this world; you stand before men.

If it comes out "Raca" you can go before the courts of the earth. But, if it comes out as "Thou fool," you'll go before God's court, because according to the Word, to say, "Thou fool" is judging a man spiritually. The Bible says, "The fool hath said in his heart, There is no God" (Ps. 14:1). So you're judging a man spiritually when you call him a fool. Today we might call him a lousy reprobate, or we might say "God's going to send you to hell for that." It is all judging the person spiritually.

It's one thing to say something against a man using earthly slander, such as Raca. It's another thing to call a man something that judges him spiritually. You're in no position to do that; God is the only one who can judge a person spiritually. "Vengeance is mine; I will repay, saith the Lord" (Rom. 12:19).

VERSE 22
But whosoever shall say, Thou fool, shall be in danger of hell fire

People often read into those verses and say, "See there, if you dare call a person a fool, you're going to hell." He didn't say that. He said if you call them a fool, that indicates you're headed in a dangerous direction.

Judge Yourself, Not Others —

In the next two verses Jesus talks about your new life before God and amplifies the term "fool."

VERSES 23,24
Therefore if thou bring thy gift to the altar, and there rememberest that thy brother hath ought against thee;

Leave there thy gift before the altar, and go thy way; first be reconciled to thy brother, and then come and offer thy gift.

Being a fool is judging someone else spiritually. When something is spiritually wrong within you — when you're out of fellowship with the Lord — it affects whatever you do spiritually. The example used in these verses is the giving of money. We know there is a blessing in giving. The Bible says, "Give, and it shall be given unto you; good measure, pressed down, shaken together, and running over shall men give into your bosom" (Luke 6:38). But will the blessing come back if you're out of fellowship with God? No. That nullifies everything.

The Word says in 1 Corinthians 13, that if you don't have love, you can bestow all your goods on the poor and it will profit you nothing. When you're out of fellowship with the Lord, everything turns into outward works. You're doing it for show; that's not the right motive. The Bible says, "Every man according as he purposeth in his heart, so let him give; not grudgingly or of necessity: for God loveth a cheerful giver" (2 Cor. 9:7).

He is talking here about a very important principle in the Word of God — judging yourself before you do anything. We saw earlier that if you don't remain pure in heart, your prayers won't work. Before you pray, make sure you're in fellowship with the Lord. Everything revolves around the principle of 1 John 1:9 in the Christian life. Make sure you're cleansed before you give. Make sure you're cleansed before you stand in faith. And, "When ye stand praying, forgive" (Mark 11:25).

Over and over again in the Word of God, it says to forgive before you do anything spiritual, and here, in verse 23 and 24 it says, before you give an offering, you are to make sure that your brother and you are reconciled.

Why would your brother have ought against you? Because you did him wrong. This didn't say he did you wrong. You did him wrong, and he has ought against you.

The next two verses talk about your life before men, and amplify the term "Raca."

VERSES 25,26
Agree with thine adversary quickly, whiles thou art in the way with him; lest at any time the adversary deliver thee to the judge, and the judge deliver thee to the officer, and thou be cast into prison.

Verily I say unto thee, thou shalt by no means come out thence, till thou hast paid the uttermost farthing.

If someone came to you and said, "I don't believe it's God's will to heal everybody; and I don't believe in all this prosperity teaching," are you supposed to agree with him? No. The term *agree* here means "come to terms." You may not agree with him, but come to terms with him. Don't argue with him. If he wants to argue with you, love him and pray for him. (Rom. 12:18.) You don't have to back down on your beliefs to come to terms.

He's saying to come to terms with your adversary (unbelievers). "Whiles thou art in the way with him" means when your paths cross — the times while you are together.

It goes on to say, "Lest at any time the adversary deliver thee to the judge, and the judge deliver thee to the officer, and thou be cast into prison." This is saying don't get cantankerous with people; don't explode at them; don't give them a piece of your mind. Why? Because that might be what they are waiting for. If they can't find any other way to put you away, they'll throw a slander suit against you for what you say. And if that happens, you might be in court for quite a while. If it goes on any further, and you get any madder at them, you might spend some time in jail, needlessly.

Let's be very clever about this. With *people*, you have to watch yourself, come to terms. But with the devil, let him have it. When he comes to your door with sickness and disease, don't try to come to terms with him, cast him out. When you run across a demon in someone, don't try to get along with it, cast it out. Use your authority.

·4

Adultery: A Sin of the Mind and the Body

Jesus talks to His disciples about another example of sin in Matthew 5:27-32. These verses amplify the seventh commandment — "Thou shalt not commit adultery." He introduces His subject in verse 27.

MATTHEW 5:27

Ye have heard that it was said by them of old time, Thou shalt not commit adultery.

Just like with murder, when Jesus mentioned adultery the disciples thought of the outward act. When you mention adultery, people usually think of two people committing illicit sex, in secret somewhere. Jesus points out what adultery is, and where it begins.

It Begins in the Mind —

VERSE 28

But I say unto you, that whosoever looketh on a woman to lust after her hath committed adultery with her already in his heart.

Adultery begins with the thoughts, not with the deed. No one who ever committed adultery just suddenly committed adultery. It started with the thought — the lust. But it didn't stop there. The devil kept using the thought until finally the outward act of adultery took place.

He didn't say it's wrong to look; He said it's wrong to *look* at a woman *to lust*. In other words, what is the intention behind the looking? Looking to lust can also be a problem for women. The reason He talked about it from a man's viewpoint here is because it is easier for a man to look to lust than a woman. Men are more enticed by the visual than are women.

If you look to lust, you've already committed adultery with the person in your heart. God sees both the act and the thought as adultery.

He didn't say looking to lust is as bad as committing adultery; He said *you have committed adultery* when you look to lust.

Cast Away Sin —

VERSES 29,30

And if thy right eye offend thee, pluck it out, and cast it from thee: for it is profitable for thee that one of thy members should perish, and not that thy whole body should be cast into hell.

And if thy right hand offend thee, cut it off, and cast it from thee: for it is profitable for thee that one of thy members should perish, and not that thy whole body should be cast into hell.

In verse 28 He said, "Whosoever looketh." You look with your eyes. Your *eyes* in verse 29 refer to *mental sins*. The *hands* in verse 30 are *outward sins* or the manifestation in the outward man. Again, He says, "If thy . . . eye offend thee, pluck it out . . . if thy . . . hand offend thee, cut it off." This is not talking about literally plucking out your eye or literally cutting off your hand. He's saying that you should be as quick to ask God to forgive you of committing a sin *mentally* as you would if you committed it *outwardly*. If most people really committed outward adultery, they would be on their knees saying, "God forgive me. God forgive me." But how often do people walk around with lust on the inside of them and keep brushing it away instead of asking for forgiveness?

The next time you get angry with someone, even light anger, imagine yourself pulling out a gun and shooting the person right in the head. Then you'll see why God says to ask for forgiveness.

He didn't say go to your *neighbor* and say, "Pluck my eye out." He didn't say ask your *neighbor*, "Cut my hand off." You pluck out your *own* eye and you cut off your *own* hand. This is an example of self-judgement. If we would judge ourselves, we would not be judged.

Jesus is pointing out that when you have a bad thought and you begin to harbor it, you need to cast it out. Bad thoughts come your way, and you can't stop them from coming. The devil *will* attack; but you don't have to receive his thoughts. You will be tempted, but if you cast temptation away, don't feel guilty that you've sinned, because you haven't. But if that thought comes along, and you begin to meditate on it, catch yourself and ask the Lord to forgive you and cast that imagination down. (2 Cor. 10:4,5.) "Pluck it out and cast it from thee."

The Word on Divorce —

VERSES 31,32

It hath been said, Whosoever shall put away his wife, let him give her a writing of divorcement:

But I say unto you, That whosoever shall put away his wife, saving for the cause of fornication, causeth her to commit adultery: and whosoever shall marry her that is divorced committeth adultery.

Jesus has identified what adultery is and how to get rid of it. In these verses, He is looking at divorce, but He is still talking about adultery.

Why was Jesus covering the subject of divorce? Because His disciples were in the dark about it.

Verse 31 says, "It hath been said. . . ." He is referring to what was said about divorce in Deuteronomy 24.

When a man hath taken a wife, and married her, and it come to pass that she find no favour in his eyes, because he hath found some uncleanness in her: then let him write her a bill of divorcement, and give it in her hand, and send her out of his house (Deut. 24:1).

By the time this verse was handed down to the disciples, it had become so perverted that men were putting away their wives for every reason imaginable, and wives were doing the same to their husbands. In fact, in Matthew 19 the disciples again came to Jesus and asked Him if it is all right to put away your wife for every reason. That question came from the confusion over what Deuteronomy 24 was saying.

The trouble began with the word "uncleanness." Under the Old Testament, there were many forms of uncleanness. If you were a leper, you were considered unclean. If you touched someone or went in the same room with someone who had a communicable disease, you were called unclean. Or, if you walked into a room where a dead body was, you were considered unclean and you had to go through purification rights to be accepted back into society.

The word *unclean* had been stretched to cover everything unclean in the Old Testament. Jesus had to come along and explain what God meant when He said unclean. God meant fornication — if a husband or wife had an affair. In this verse, we're talking about the wife, but it also worked the other way around: If a man was considered unclean, she could write him a bill of divorcement.

If a man married a woman and she had an affair and he wrote her a bill of divorcement, which one of them would be at fault? In this example, the *woman* would be at fault. He found an uncleanness in *her* according to the way Jesus defined uncleanness. Fornication is the outward sexual act. She is the one who committed fornication against him. He had a legitimate right to put her away. Now, if that woman would have been in most churches today, she would have been condemned out the door.

What about Remarrying? —

Would she have been allowed to remarry in most churches today? No. But look at what Deuteronomy 24:2 says about that. "And when she is departed (*the guilty one*) out of his house, she may go and be another man's wife." The Word says she can remarry.

Look at verses 3 and 4. "And if the latter husband hate her, and write her a bill of divorcement, and giveth it in her hand and sendeth her out of the house; or if the latter husband die, which took her to be his wife; Her former husband, which sent her away, may not take her again to be his wife, after that she is defiled; for that is abomination before the Lord." Notice it says, her former husband which sent her away may not take her again to be his wife after that she is defiled.

A man came to me for counseling and said, "I want you to agree with me that my wife is going to come back." He had had an affair and when his wife found out about it, she went out and had an affair. They both got mad, split up over it and got a divorce.

I said, "Well okay, let's put our faith together on the Word." As we talked further, I asked, "Where is she right now?"

"Oh, she's remarried," he said.

49

I said, "Forget it."

"No. God saw our marriage," he said, "and He doesn't recognize this marriage."

I told him, "No, you're wrong. God does recognize divorce. He doesn't like it, but He does recognize it. Divorce is a sin in the Word of God. Now, if you will confess your sin, He's faithful and just to forgive you of your sin, and cleanse you from all unrighteousness. You are free to get married again. You are praying for her to *sin* by praying for her to get a divorce and come back to you. God *does* recognize her new marriage and does not want you to marry her again. God sees *you* as free to remarry.

We saw where remarriage was allowed in the Old Testament; now let's look at it in the New Testament. Look at 1 Corinthians 7:27. "Art thou bound unto a wife? seek not to be loosed. Art thou loosed from a wife? seek not a wife." The word *bound* here means married. He says, "Don't seek to be loosed." Don't look to divorce. Divorce is not the answer. If divorce seems like the answer, do whatever it takes to make the matter right.

Are you divorced from a wife? Seek not a wife; don't make that your goal. What are you to do? Seek after the kingdom of God, and these things will be added unto you. (Matt. 6:33.) Put the Lord first and His kingdom, and God will see that the right one comes across your path.

He continues, "But and if thou marry, thou hast not sinned" (1 Cor. 7:28). Remarriage is not a sin.

Divorce Causes Adultery —

VERSE 32

But I say unto you, That whosoever shall put away his wife, saving for the cause of fornication. . . .

Notice that He said, "for the cause of fornication" — not adultery. He has switched from talking about adultery to talking about fornication. The wording is specific here. He has just been saying that adultery can be in the thoughts, and adultery can be manifested in the outward conduct. But, when He comes over to a reason for divorce, He switches to fornication. Why? Because He's just defined adultery; if He used the word *adultery* they might think they could put away their wives for meditating on bad thoughts. So He switches to fornication. He is saying only the outward act is a reason for divorce.

". . . causeth her to commit adultery — (v. 32).

He goes back to the word adultery. Is this saying she went to bed with someone? No, it's talking about another kind of adultery.

Spiritual Union Divided —

Now we can get into the very important roots of what this verse is saying: Marriage is deeper than the flesh; it gets into the inner man. Marriage is not just the union of two bodies, it is the union of two spirits.

"Yes, but the Bible says that if any two shall become married, they'll become one flesh," someone says.

The Bible also says it's not right for a believer to marry an unbeliever. (2 Cor. 6:14.) If marriage was just two bodies joined together, what difference would it make to marry an unbeliever? My body is like an unbeliever's body, it didn't change in salvation. It was my inner man that changed. That verse goes on to say, "What communion hath light with darkness? And what concord hath Christ with Belial (*or the devil*)?" Light and darkness are the *inner man*, not the outer man. God does not live in my body, He lives in my spirit; therefore the devil doesn't live in the unbeliever's body, he lives in his spirit.

When two people get married, they are joined deeper than just the body; their spirits are joined together. When

God speaks to married people who are both walking in fellowship with Him, He doesn't speak to one, He speaks to both, because God sees them as united. They are still two *individuals*, but God sees them as operating as one; and their two spirits begin to flow together as one. It's just like when you were born again. Your spirit and God are two separate spirits, but they joined together in unity.

When a husband and wife are joined together in the spirit, it is difficult to tear them apart. It's difficult because the Lord sees you as two *spirits*. Divorce is not just two *bodies* going their own ways; it's two *spirits* being torn apart. *Adultery* here isn't talking about outward adultery; it's talking about spiritual separation.

When a man puts away his wife for a reason other than a Biblical reason, he is causing their two spirits to be torn apart and causing an adultery within the woman for which she didn't ask.

One of the hardest things also in a person's life is remarriage. Can it be done? Yes, it can; but it takes a lot of time, a lot of love, and a lot of patience; but it can be worked out. A spirit separated from one can be joined to another. There are a lot of hurts and pains to be overcome, but God's Word and the Holy Spirit can heal them all.

5

Swear Not

MATTHEW 5:33-35

Again, ye have heard that it hath been said by them of old time, Thou shalt not forswear thyself, but shalt perform unto the Lord thine oaths:

But I say unto you, swear not at all; neither by heaven; for it is God's throne.

Nor by the earth, for it is his footstool: neither by Jerusalem; for it is the city of the great King.

Jesus says, "Don't forswear yourself." Now, immediately when I say "Don't forswear yourself," the first thing people usually think about is cursing — swearing. You say, "Well, that verse doesn't apply to me because I don't curse; I don't swear; I don't use profanity."

That is not what He is talking about here at all. Forswearing means to take an oath or a vow.

To forswear yourself is to pull something into your conversation which is bigger than you are, to prop up your statement because in and of itself your statement was weak. When people pull something into their statement, it's always bigger than they are.

"Swear not at all, neither by heaven for it is God's throne." That means saying something like, "Oh, as the heavens are above me, I promise to keep my word." He says, "Nor by the earth." You didn't have anything to do with making the earth, yet people back in Jesus' day would swear by the earth, such as saying, "As the earth is below me, I swear I'll do it."

"Neither by Jerusalem, for it is the city of the great King." They would swear by the great city of Jerusalem because that's where the King was going to rule and reign for a thousand years in His kingdom.

VERSE 36

Neither shalt thou swear by thy head, because thou canst not make one hair white or black.

Why would you swear by your head? Because in your head is probably the most intricate part of your body — the brain. They'd swear by their heads. They didn't have anything to do with creating a brain.

I know what you are thinking: "That's silly. I would never do that. Cross my heart." You just swore by your heart.

VERSE 37

But let your communication be yea, yea; Nay, nay: for whatsoever is more than these cometh of evil.

When you say yes, mean yes; and when you say no, mean no. The next time you start to say yes, and you're going to take on the end of it, "as God is my witness," just remember who told you to say that — the devil. Jesus said, "Whatsoever is more than your yes or more than your no cometh from *the evil one*." The devil wants you to prop up your statements because it makes you look weak in yourself. You don't need to pull in God to prop up your statement. Just let your own character be strong enough. It's the Holy Spirit in you who prompts you to say yes or no and mean it.

Immediately the question arises, "But what if I have to go to court? What if someone wants me to testify on their behalf, and I have to put my hand on the Bible? Do I need to do that?" The answer is yes, do it. You're not doing it for *your* benefit; you're doing it for *their* benefit. They want to know if you will put your hand on a Bible. If that is what they need, fine; I'll put my hand on a Bible for their sake, but I don't need to because I would tell the truth anyway. Sure, the Bible is the Word of God, but it's just a book; and you're just laying a physical hand on a physical book. I'm not telling the truth because that book is in *front* of me; I'm telling the truth because Jesus Christ lives *in* me. The important thing is not the book, it's what the book says and what I have hidden in my heart so that I might not sin against Him.

God's Word to *us* is always yes or no. He needs nothing else to prop up His statements. We also should let our yes or no stand alone. (2 Cor. 1:17-20.)

6

Should Christians Retaliate?

Most Christians have heard the terms "An eye for an eye," and "Turn the other cheek." But the verses are often quoted out of context, and most really don't know what they mean. Knowing when to "turn the other cheek," and when to take up for yourself often presents a problem for the Christian who is trying to walk in love. In Matthew 5:38-48, Jesus tells us about Christian retaliation.

MATTHEW 5:38

Ye have heard that it hath been said, An eye for an eye, and a tooth for a tooth.

This is quoted from the Old Testament: Exodus 21:24, Leviticus 24:20 and Deuteronomy 19:21. If you'll look at those verses in context, you'll see that the quote was not written for the Christian's walk; it's directed toward a judge who sits at the bench and makes a decision in a courtroom. This is how judges decided the penalty for crimes committed. If somebody was brought into the courtroom, the law the judge went by was that if the defendant had knocked out someone's tooth, he would get his tooth knocked out. And if he gouged out someone's eye, the court would remove his eye. It was pretty simple for a judge to officiate over a courtroom. He didn't have to listen to all the motives and details behind the crime.

The judge would say, "What happened? Did you punch his eye out?"

"Yes," would respond the defendant.

57

"Punch his eye out. Case dismissed. Next case."

So, this statement was not directed toward the people of the city; it was directed toward a certain group of individuals — judges. But, men had pulled that scripture out of context and were applying it to circumstances of life. They thought if someone came and did something evil to you, you had all the rights to go and return it to them.

Turn the Other Cheek —

VERSE 39

But I say unto you, That ye resist not evil: but whosoever shall smite thee on thy right cheek, turn to him the other also.

This verse was not directed to all people, but to certain ones. Church religious leaders today read it and they want to apply it to all cases. If we look back to the Beatitudes, we can see the context in which Jesus is speaking. Remember verse 10 was the Beatitude of maturity because it talks about being able to rejoice in the midst of persecution. In it Jesus says, "Blessed are they which are persecuted for righteousness' sake."

He is saying "When persecution comes *for my sake*." When a lot of people read "turn to him the other (cheek) also," they immediately get a complex that Christians always ought to go around being a "punching bag" for the world: You should be weak and spineless. The world can take away everything you have, and you should stand there and grin. That's not what this verse is saying.

Jesus is talking about your stand for the *gospel*. When you are being persecuted, you do not retaliate "for my sake." The time He is talking about is when men shall revile you for *righteousness*' sake. Fists are not the way we defend the gospel. If someone comes up and slaps you because you're a *Christian*, fists are not the way to respond. He says, "Don't

58

resist evil." The word *evil* again refers to the evil one. It's not a *person* slapping you on the other cheek, it's the *evil one*. But the devil is not coming against you; he's coming against Jesus in you. We don't fight the devil with fists. The Bible says, "Vengeance is mine; I will repay, saith the Lord" (Rom. 12:19).

Give Him Your Cloak Also —

VERSE 40

And if any man will sue thee at the law, and take away thy coat, let him have thy cloak also."

This verse is not referring to natural cases but to being sued for the gospel's sake, for righteousness' sake. Some people would love to haul you to court, and they are going to try to find ways to do it.

Jesus was saying, "Whenever they sue you for one thing, give them something better or give them more than they asked for." Why? We don't retaliate with fists, we retaliate with love. Love will accomplish a lot more than fists will. A fist just knocks them out for a while. Love will keep them confused for a long time.

Some Christians think you should never go to court for any reason, but we're talking about going to court *because* of the gospel. Courts are not the way to settle things between Christians. (1 Cor. 6:1-8.)

But when things *not* pertaining to the gospel happen, there are laws to protect us. That's what they are there for, and we can use them. In fact, Romans 13 tells us the government is set up by God and is there to help you in cases of natural things.

A person who was attending a Bible school came to me and told me that he had taken his car into a garage to have some carburetor work done on it. When he went to pick

59

it up, the whole side of his car was smashed in. He asked the man about the damage, and the man said, "Oh well, we took it out for a test drive, and we wrecked it."

He said, "What are you going to do about it?" The man said, "Nothing. It's your car, and you put it in here at your own risk."

He looked at me, "Should I do something about that?"

"This has *nothing* to do with your stand for the gospel. This man is trying to take advantage of you. The devil would love to take everything you have and get you so in debt over that car that you couldn't afford to go to school." Then I gave him the name of a good Christian lawyer to call and find out just what he could do. So, you can see where we're dividing the spiritual from the natural.

VERSE 41

And whosoever shall compel thee to go a mile, go with him twain.

While the last verse was talking about Christians, this one refers to the world. The outside world at the time that Jesus was preaching the Sermon on the Mount was the Roman Empire. When He talks about sinners and the outside world, He usually is referring to the Romans. The Romans could have cared less about the Jews' religion. The Romans had their own religion.

The only thing the Romans wanted to do with the Jews was to use them. One way was to grab a Jew who was standing by the side of the road and make him carry the soldier's heavy pack for a mile. Usually the Jew would take the pack on his back and complain every step of that mile. He would keep glaring at that Roman and if looks could kill, he'd be dead. He'd walk along murmuring under his breath, and as soon as they would get to the end of the mile where the mile marker stops, he would throw down the pack, probably spit on it and walk off. The Roman would pick it up and go along and find another Jew to carry it.

The Jews were compelled by law to carry it for a mile.

Matthew 27:31,32 shows this practice. This is when they were going to crucify Jesus. "And after they had mocked him, they took the robe off from him, and put his own raiment on him, and led him away to crucify him. And as they came out, they found a man of Cyrene, Simon by name: him they *compelled* to bear his cross." Notice, they "compelled" him to carry the cross.

But Jesus said, "And whosoever shall compel thee to go a mile, go with him twain." Suppose that you're standing at the side of the road, and a soldier comes along and puts his pack on you and says, "Carry it." So, you start carrying it for a mile. With the first mile, he's got you; he's talking to you and probably laughing at you, and ribbing you, because by law you're compelled to carry that pack.

As you approach the end of that mile, he's expecting you to walk up to the mile marker and throw it down; but instead, he sees your feet keep right on going, and you walk the second mile. Suddenly, that guy who did all the talking for the first mile shuts up and looks at you. Now it's your turn. You've got him. For one mile *he had you*, but for the next mile *you have him*. By the time you get to the end of the second mile, the man will probably be on his knees accepting Jesus. Why? What did it? Love. The Bible says, ". . . the goodness of God leadeth thee to repentance" (Rom. 2:4).

Many grew up on hell, fire and brimstone teachings, and a few people will get saved that way. (Jude 23.) But have you noticed how many people are getting born again today — they are being swept in by the masses — and it's the love of God and the goodness of God that is bringing them into the kingdom. That is what Jesus is saying here. You know

the old expression is true: You can draw more flies with
honey than you can with vinegar. That's true with the gospel.

Give to Those Who Ask —

VERSE 42

Give to him that asketh thee, and from him that
would borrow of thee turn not thou away.

Your Christian witness extends into the area of
borrowing and lending. It is not wrong to borrow, and it
is not wrong to lend. That was not Jesus' issue at all. The
point is, when someone wants to borrow some money from
you, go ahead and lend it to them. That's part of your
Christian witness.

He isn't saying for you to give to everyone who comes
around because you also have to save some for yourself. The
Bible says that if you don't provide for your own family,
you're worse than an infidel. (1 Tim. 5:8.) You have to know
where the balance is in this verse.

Love Thy Neighbor —

VERSE 43

Ye have heard that it hath been said, Thou shalt
love thy neighbour, and hate thine enemy.

The religious leaders had added that last half of that
verse, because that is not what Leviticus 19:18 says, It says,
". . . thou shalt love thy neighbour *as thyself.*" It doesn't say
"And hate thine enemy." They just switched it around and
assumed that if you are to love your neighbor, then
apparently you can hate your enemies.

Where they missed it was on the word *neighbor.* For the
word *neighbor,* the religious leaders interpreted it as *friend,*
so as to mean, "Love your friends."

Jesus points out that your neighbor is not just your friend; your neighbor can be an enemy — one who doesn't like you. He said that you're supposed to pour out the same love on your friends and on your enemies because they are all your neighbors.

Love Your Enemies Also —

VERSES 44,45

But I say unto you, Love your enemies, bless them that curse you, do good to them that hate you, and pray for them which despitefully use you, and persecute you;

That ye may be the children of your Father which is in heaven: for he maketh his sun to rise on the evil and on the good, and sendeth rain on the just and on the unjust.

This does not say that you are not going to heaven if you don't love everyone. That is not what determines whether or not you're born again. You're born again because you accept the lordship of Jesus. What we're dealing with here is maturity.

There are two Greek words for *children: teknon* which means "child," and *huios* which means "sons." Huios indicates maturity. You are a *teknon*, but you grow into a *huios* through the Word of God. This verse should be translated, "That ye may *become* the *sons* of your Father which is in heaven."

It's not talking about whether or not you're a child of God. It's talking about whether or not you're a *son* of God, an *adult* of God. You don't become an adult overnight. The moment you are born again, you are not a son of God; you are a child of God. You *become* a son of God. When you become the son of your Father, or become mature, you start imitating your Father.

In my early teen years, I was amazed at how dumb my parents appeared to be. We didn't think anything alike. But it's amazing how mature my parents got as I entered my twenties. They grew up so fast! We started thinking alike. What happened? The change wasn't in them, it was in me. As I got older, I began to find out that they really were smart, and they really did know what they were talking about. I started acting more like them.

Many times in the Christian life, we see that the Word says something, but we think we know better. We think God doesn't know the twentieth century; He's speaking to people back in the old times. Things have changed. That's wrong. The Bible is the same yesterday, today and forever. God's Word is not going to change. It is going to have to be you who changes and gets in line with that Word. The moment you do, you will start acting like God. Maturity comes in when you start acting like your heavenly Father.

God is no respecter of persons; He loves everyone. He sends the sun and the rain on both the good and the bad. Your love should be like the sun and the rain, and just fall on everyone. If they slap you because you're a Christian, just keep loving them. If they want to haul you to court, just keep loving them. If they want you to go one mile, go two and love them. Don't let your love be partial.

VERSE 46

For if ye love them which love you, what reward have ye? do not even the publicans the same?

Publicans were considered the lowest people in society; they were tax collectors. They worked for the Roman government; yet, they were Jews.

Rome hired the tax collectors and told them, "We demand 20 percent of the people's income."

The tax collector would say, "Fine," and go to the Jew and say, "Give it over, buddy; 30 percent."

"Isn't that a little high?" the Jew would question.

"No," the tax collector would respond, "give it here or I'll have you arrested. If you don't pay, I'll turn you over to the Roman government." So the Jew would give him 30 percent, and the tax collector would give the government 20 percent and keep the other 10 percent for himself.

Therefore, tax collectors were rich, and they lived in the nicest homes at the people's expense.

If you just love those who love you, you are no better than the unbeliever. Where is the supernatural in that? God's love is supernatural. Loving those who hate you is God's love. Only His sons and daughters can do *that*.

VERSES 47,48

And if ye salute your brethren only, what do ye
more than others? do not even the publicans so?
Be ye therefore perfect, even as your Father which
is in heaven is perfect.

The word *perfect* means "mature." The whole issue here is maturity. Becoming a son is a process, and it does not come overnight. Learn to imitate your Father, God.

God's love is unchangeable; He always gives. He did the most for you when you were a sinner; He gave you salvation. Could He do any less for you now that you're born again? It's just God's nature to give; and He wants you to act like He does. He wants you to become mature in the Word of God so it's your nature to give. Give your love freely to all people whether they are good or evil.

7

Carnal Christians

We have come to a pivotal point in the Sermon on the Mount. We are coming to Matthew 6, which talks about doing a good thing with the wrong motive. But, to understand chapter 6, we first need to look at 1 Corinthians 3 which deals with an area in the Christian life that very few people know or teach about because they don't understand it — being a carnal Christian.

In verse 1, Paul says to the Corinthians, *"And I, brethren."* Is he speaking to believers or unbelievers? Believers; you wouldn't call sinners "brethren." So, he is talking to born-again Christians. Since he starts it out that way, people immediately think he's going to be talking to great spiritual people. Well, let's find out what he said to them.

1 Corinthians 3:1

And I, brethren, could not speak unto you as unto spiritual, but as unto carnal, even as unto babes in Christ.

That verse of scripture blows many doctrines and teachings we have today because some people can't understand how you can be a Christian and be carnal at the same time. Those two words don't seem to go together — *carnal* and *Christian*.

The church has been divided into two camps for years: Both of them have had a hard time realizing the fact that Christians sin. When they see someone do something wrong, they go and tell everyone, "Did you hear what brother so-and-so did?" And everyone says, "No." So they say, "He did thus and thus." The other person then says, "He did? Why, I thought he was saved!"

So, immediately, two camps arise. One camp says, "He's lost his salvation." The other camp says, "He was never saved in the first place."

Both of them are wrong. If he accepted Jesus Christ as his Savior, he is born again, but sinned. That doesn't mean he's not a Christian, that means as 1 Corinthians, chapter 3, says, he is a carnal Christian, a babe in Christ.

When we get born again, the issue is not sin. Despite what people have said for years, the issue for the unbeliever is not his sins, it's a matter of accepting the lordship of Jesus.

However, once a person is born again, sin *does* become an issue. Jesus entrusts the believer with the responsibility of handling his own sin. He is now a new creation and the Holy Spirit living inside of him makes him big enough to handle it. Again we get back into the two camps. If a believer sins, is that sin going to separate him from his relationship with the Lord Jesus? No. It wasn't giving up sin that got him in God's family in the first place.

First Corinthians is not discussing relationship. He called them brethren, and that indicates they are in relationship with the Lord. But the fact that he calls them "carnal" and "babes" indicates they are out of fellowship. In verse 1, he said, "I could not speak to you as unto spiritual." So, being in fellowship is being spiritual, and being out of fellowship is being carnal.

Spiritual Babies —

Paul calls them spiritual babies or carnal Christians. Let's look at some characteristics of spiritual babies.

VERSE 2

I have fed you with milk, and not with meat: for hitherto ye were not able to bear it, neither yet now are ye able.

One of the first characteristics of spiritual babies, as well as natural babies, is they need milk. If you feed a natural baby milk, he will grow up. The Bible says, "As newborn babes, desire the sincere milk of the word, that ye may *grow* thereby" (1 Pet. 2:2). Milk develops in you a hunger and a thirst for more food, for a bigger variety of food. There is milk in the Word of God that we need to feed spiritual babies, so they will begin to develop a hunger and thirst for more of the Word of God.

You never lose your appetite for milk. I enjoy a glass of milk once in a while, but not all the time. The same thing is true about spiritual things. I enjoy going back and just hearing the basics once in a while, but that doesn't mean that it is my steady diet. But, babies need milk all the time; they can't get into deeper things of the Word of God.

Another sign of a spiritual baby is that babies demand attention. It's a sure way to spot them in a congregation: They love to be called on; they love to stand up and have people look at them. Now, there's nothing wrong with recognizing people in church, but if a person can't do his work as unto the Lord, then I, personally, don't want him to do it. You have to give babies attention sometimes, but at the same time you should be giving them food so they will grow out of that stage. Attention is all right in small quantities, but you should know where to draw the line.

Babies like entertainment. You cannot hold a baby's attention by talking to him. Lean over a crib sometime and try talking to a baby; it won't get you anywhere. Unless you stick your fingers in your ears, cross your eyes and stick out your tongue, you cannot hold a baby's attention. Babies are that way in a congregation too; unless you have entertainment every Sunday night, they'll pack up their marbles and go somewhere else.

In this passage of scripture we're not talking so much about the babies who have just been born again, we're talking about people who have been saved for 20 or 30 years and have never grown up. They come to church infrequently; they sit back and sulk and won't listen. Then they go home and criticize the pastor and members of the congregation. They all are out of fellowship with the Lord. They have done things wrong; they won't admit it, and they won't get back into fellowship with God. So they continue in strife, envy and every kind of sin.

People who are out of fellowship with the Lord *cannot* grow. But if you are in fellowship with the Lord, you can grow. Notice I said, "You *can* grow." There's no guarantee that you *will* grow. Just being in fellowship with the Lord doesn't mean you will grow. There are two prerequisites for growing which are found in John 15:7. Number one is, "If ye abide in me." That is fellowship. Prerequisite number two is, "and my words abide in you." You must be in fellowship with the Lord and taking in His Word to grow. As you grow, the Word of God will build up your defenses and help you to resist the temptation to sin. As you continue to grow, resisting the devil will get easier and easier for you.

Carnal Corinth —

Now we would immediately surmise in 1 Corinthians 3:1,2 that the Corinthians to whom Paul was writing were guilty of terrible sins. Corinth was probably one of the hardest places to get a church going in the ancient world. It was a pleasure city. Getting them born again and into the kingdom of God was easy, because it wasn't a religious city, but renewing their minds was difficult. They were so ingrained with sex and having a wild time that they'd get born again and say, "Let's just keep on having a wild time." They had sexual problems. A man was caught in adultery in the church, and yet the church was letting it go on. Why?

Because they were accustomed to it. So Paul had to start teaching them about morality. Salvation was not the issue, the issue was getting them in line with the Word of God.

Did you know that you can be born again and be just as carnal as these Corinthians were and still operate in the gifts of the Spirit? They did. Spiritual gifts were rampant in their church. But there was no order because they were so used to going to the extreme in everything. So, Paul had to come along and define how to get things in order.

So Paul directs his remarks to those who are born again but who are still babies.

VERSE 3

For ye are yet carnal: for whereas there is among you envying, and strife, and divisions, are ye not carnal, and walk as men?

What caused all the *outward* sins? It was all the *inward* sins. What's on the inside will manifest itself on the outside.

The Amplified translation says, walk "like *mere* . . . men." When you are out of fellowship with the Lord or carnal long enough, you will look and act like an unbeliever. You get as mad as an unbeliever; you get just as frustrated and upset. You look like a "mere man."

When you're out of fellowship, you're not under control of the Holy Spirit. If you are not under the control of the Holy Spirit, you are under the control of the flesh. There is only one way to get back under the control of the Spirit and that is 1 John 1:9.

Reaping the Reward —

If you are out of fellowship, carnal, you can pray, give money, go to church, or work for the Lord, but it will not count. God says there are *rewards* laid up for you. But what kind of rewards are we discussing? Look at 1 Corinthians 3:8.

71

VERSE 8

Now he that planteth and he that watereth are one:
and every man shall receive his own reward
according to his own labour.

He says you are responsible for your own rewards; they
will be determined by your labor. Notice that laboring doesn't
have anything to do with the new birth; laboring has to do
with *rewards*. He didn't say, "According to your labors will
you go to heaven." He says, "According to your labors will
you receive rewards."

So, the object in my Christian life is not to get to heaven.
I am not striving to go to heaven, I am striving in the
Christian life to get more rewards when I get to heaven. Not
only will I get rewards when I get to heaven; I'm also going
to get rewards down here.

I can stop my rewards here and cease my rewards in
heaven by getting out of fellowship with the Lord. Faith won't
work out of fellowship with the Lord.

VERSES 9-11

For we are labourers together with God: ye are
God's husbandry, ye are God's building.

According to the grace of God which is given unto
me, as a wise masterbuilder, I have laid the
foundation, and another man buildeth thereon. But
let every man take heed how he buildeth
thereupon.

For other foundation can no man lay than that is
laid, which is Jesus Christ.

The Bible says that Jesus Christ is "the foundation that
was laid" in your Christian life. Paul was saying, "I laid it,
but you built on it." Every born-again Christian received the
foundation in his life, because someone preached the Word

72

of God. We took in the foundation — Jesus Christ — but once the foundation was there, it was up to us to build upon it.

How are you building upon your foundation? How you build upon it is going to determine your rewards in heaven. When we get to heaven, the Lord is going to judge our works. The Bible says that when we get to heaven, we're all going to differ as stars in magnitude. (1 Cor. 15:41,42.) That means we'll differ according to what we did in life with the Word of God, how we reacted with the Word of God, and how we built our life. I don't want to go to heaven and be a star that twinkles now and then. I want to go to heaven and be a supernova for the Lord. I want to have tremendous rewards when I get there. So, I'm going to make sure that in my lifetime I am in fellowship when I do anything for the Lord.

VERSE 12

Now if any man build upon this foundation gold, silver, precious stones, wood, hay, stubble.

How do we distinguish between gold, silver, precious stones, wood, hay, and stubble? Let me give you an example. A married couple got up one morning and things weren't going very well. As she was making breakfast, the phone rang, and she answered it. When she turned back to the stove, the eggs were fried crisp and black and the biscuits looked like charcoal. She got mad and frustrated. When the husband came in, instead of trying to smooth things over, he got mad and piled on more condemnation. They were going to church; so they got into the car. She decided she was wrong and apologized to him. He chewed her out some more. She quietly prayed, "Lord, forgive me. According to 1 John 1:9, I confess that sin. I know You're faithful and just to forgive me of that sin, and so Father, I stand cleansed before You." When they got to church, she was in fellowship with God, but he was not. He's carnal and she's spiritual.

At church, the pastor announced that a missionary had suddenly run into some extreme difficulty and needed a certain amount of money. The church was going to take up an offering for him that morning. When the offering bucket was passed, the man and his wife each put in $100.

God saw both of them give. But, one was giving *in* fellowship, and one was giving *out* of fellowship. We couldn't go to the man and say, "You sinned giving that money." Giving an offering is good. What counts is the *motivation* behind giving the money. Why did *he* give, and why did *she* give?

He might think that $100 will somehow excuse his unforgiveness; that God is a big softheart and can be bought off. Also that the offering will cover his guilt. God looks at the intent of the heart. Both of them have a foundation, but on her foundation she piled $100 worth of gold, silver and precious stones. He just piled up $100 worth of wood, hay and stubble. They both gave $100, but the intent of the heart was different with both.

What should he have done?

When he saw the bucket coming, he should have thought, "Wait a minute, let me examine myself; is there anything wrong? Yes, there is. I argued with my wife this morning, and I'm still holding a grudge against her. Father, as I drop my money in there, I'm going to ask you to forgive me according to 1 John 1:9, I confess my sins. I know You're faithful to forgive me of my sins and to cleanse me from all unrighteousness. I now ask You to forgive me, and I'm going to ask my wife to forgive me later." Immediately God sees his offering switch from wood, hay and stubble to gold, silver and precious stones.

As you look back over your Christian life, there are probably times you have not received gold, silver and precious stones. There have been times you piled up wood, hay and stubble. If you've been out of fellowship with the Lord for a month or two months, and all that time you still did the same things you did when you were in fellowship, you were piling up wood, hay and stubble. You still gave money; you still prayed; you might have fasted and said all the right things; yet on the inside something was different. You were not saying and doing things out of the energy of the spirit, but out of the energy of the flesh to try to appease your guilt complex. You know what God sees when you do that — wood, hay and stubble.

VERSE 13

Every man's work shall be made manifest: for the day shall declare it.

The "day" represents the judgement seat of Christ. This is not talking about the great white throne judgement — that is for sinners. It's talking about the judgement seat of Christ where all Christians will stand before God and their works will be made manifest before Him. (2 Cor. 5:10). Verse 13 goes on to say:

. . . because it shall be revealed by fire; and the fire shall try every man's works of what sort it is.

It didn't say the fire is going to try *you*; it is going to try your *works*.

VERSE 14

If any man's work abide which he hath built thereupon, he shall receive a reward.

That is one of the most glorious scriptures in the Word of God. It says that the wood, hay and stubble are not going to be held against you. When the fire hits the foundation, will the foundation be burned? No, because the foundation is Jesus Christ. Will the gold, silver and precious stones be burned? No. What is going to be burned is the wood, hay and stubble. That which is burned up is not going to be held against you, but you will be rewarded for what's *left over*.

The next question that arises is, "What if after it's all over and the smoke and the dust settle, I've got the biggest bonfire of anyone, and all I ever did was build wood, hay and stubble all my life? What's going to happen to me? Am I going to be cast into hell?" The answer is no.

VERSE 15

If any man's work shall be burned, he shall suffer loss: but he himself shall be saved; yet so as by fire.

What you end up with is a person who is born again, *period*. That is all he has. He has the new birth and nothing else. All his lifetime, he piled up wood, hay and stubble and nothing else. He is up in heaven where there are no more tears and all the former things are passed away. But I don't want to just be in heaven. I want to be there with a lot of rewards. I will take the Word, act upon it and remain in fellowship with the Lord and build upon the foundation gold, silver and precious stones.

Jesus said that even a cup of cold water given in His name will be rewarded. It's not the quantity; it's the quality of your giving. You can give one million dollars and be out of fellowship with the Lord, and it's nothing in God's eyes; it's wood, hay and stubble which will be burned up. But you can give a cup of cold water in His name in fellowship with the Lord and out of love, and its's gold, silver and precious stones.

8

Give as You Purpose in Your Heart

In Matthew 6, Jesus leaves the subject of sin which He covered in the previous chapter and begins talking about good things: giving, praying, fasting, and riches. Verse 1 introduces the theme of the whole chapter.

MATTHEW 6:1

Take heed that ye do not your alms before men, to be seen by them: otherwise ye have no reward of your Father which is in heaven.

The word for "alms" in this verse is *righteousness*, which refers to righteous acts or righteous deeds. "Make sure that you don't do your *righteous deeds* before men to be seen of them, otherwise you have no reward of your Father which is in heaven."

Giving Is a Righteous Act —

VERSE 2

Therefore when thou doest thine alms, do not sound a trumpet before thee, as the hypocrites do in the synagogues and in the streets, that they may have glory of men. Verily I say unto you, They have their reward.

The trumpet here is not an analogy, it is literal. In the time of Jesus, the scribes and Pharisees sounded a trumpet to demand everyone's attention as they gave their money.

Many of them carried their own brass band around with them on the streets and in the synagogues.

When they sounded the trumpets, everyone would look at them, and then they would drop their money into the offering. They would give large amounts. Someone would say, "Did you see that?" and the scribe or Pharisee would say, "Look, that's not all." And he would put in more. Everyone around would say, "Oh, did you see that?"

God says, "Yes, I saw that all right — wood, hay, stubble."

"Yes, but he gave $500,000. Did you see that?"

God says, "It's nothing. He is out of fellowship with Me. He's doing it to be seen of men and to get the rewards of men. As far as I'm concerned, it counts nothing."

If that man was saved, his offering was wood, hay, and stubble. If he was not saved, it was nothing. He can't buy his way into heaven.

The amount doesn't make the difference, the important thing is in the heart.

Not as the Hypocrites —

The word *hypocrite* is very interesting. It comes from the word *hupokrites*, a word used in the Greek theater. If you've ever been to an old theater, you've probably seen the two masks they used; one has a big smile which represents comedy, and one has a big frown and represents tragedy. If the scene was a tragedy, the actors would put the big frown over their face so everyone in the audience could see it was a tragedy. They would put the mask with the big smile on it over their face to make sure everyone would know when it was a comedy. The person who spoke from behind the mask was called a *hypocrite*. The word hypocrite literally means "to speak from behind the mask." It means that the person behind the mask is different than the mask.

He's following the same theme He discussed in Matthew 5 — that religious people always put on a facade. They say, "I'd never kill anyone," yet, on the inside, they are full of envy, strife, and division. They are harboring unforgiveness on the inside, and on the outside they have a beautiful smile on their face.

The hypocrites He is speaking about are the religious people. Religious people today are both believers and unbelievers. A lot of believers turn religious after they get born again, and they do everything for the outward show. They are the people who will stand in heaven with just a lot of dust and smoke because all they ever did in their lifetime was pile up wood, hay, and stubble. Their whole Christian life might be a series of bounding in and out of fellowship, but they never did anything for the Lord out of the right motive.

"Well, I'd never sound a trumpet," someone says.

Yes, but you've probably waved that bill around so everyone could see it before you gave it.

Jesus refers to two specific places in this verse: the synagogues and the streets. Synagogues are where the religious people are, and the street is where the world is. Hypocrites don't care whether they are seen of Christians or sinners, as long as they are seen. If you are giving to be seen of men, their praise is all the reward you are going to get.

VERSES 3,4

But when thou doest alms, let not thy left hand know what thy right hand doeth: That thine alms may be in secret: and thy Father which seeth in secret himself shall reward thee openly.

This is an *analogy*. For your left hand to know what your right hand is doing, your left hand would have to have brains and it doesn't. Do it in secret. If they happen to see, that's fine; but don't do it so anyone will see you.

Does it say that it is wrong to give in front of men? No. It says don't do it in front of men *to be seen of them*. There are times when the Spirit of the Lord moves for people to stand up and give a certain amount. But, think about why you are standing up. Are you being pressured because everyone around you is giving so much, and you think, *Oh, I better give. They'll think I'm bad if I don't give a certain amount*. So, you stand up so everyone around you will think great of you. They don't think great of you; you are just part of the crowd. But, to you, it's important that people *see* you give. If that's your motive, sure someone got your money. That church might be built or whatever, but you did it for the wrong reason.

I was in a service where the Spirit of God began to move, and the speaker said, "God wants you to give. In fact, He wants you to run up here and throw the money on the platform." I saw the Spirit of God move so much that people literally jumped out of their seats, ran to the front, and threw their money on the platform. That was the Spirit of God. I had never been to a service like that. You certainly couldn't say that that was wrong.

But, there are always a few who get with the excitement of the thing, and they think maybe they should give. God will sometimes impress you and say to give a certain amount. Respond to Him and do it. But if He doesn't move, sometimes it's all right not to give. But if you do want to give, then the Bible says, "Every man according as *he purposeth* in his heart, so let him give; not grudgingly, or of necessity" (2 Cor. 9:7). Ask yourself the questions, "Am I giving this grudgingly? Am I being pressured to give this?" If the answers are no, then give as you purpose in your heart:

Set a figure in your heart and give it. When you give it, don't do it just to be seen by men around you; do it because you want to please the Lord. If that's the motive behind it, you're not only laying up gold, silver and precious stones in heaven, you're insuring that it's going to come back to you on every wave in this life.

The Secret Place —

"That thine alms may be in secret: and thy Father which seeth in secret himself shall reward thee openly." Where is this place he calls "secret?" Remember verse 1 said, "... your Father which is in *heaven*." Notice that your Father is in heaven. Man looks on the outward appearance, but God looks on the heart. God is a spirit, and He sees in the spirit realm. The word *secret* here means the spirit realm, because your Father which is in secret is your Father which is in heaven, or the spirit realm.

If you purpose in your heart to give, God who lives in the spirit realm and sees in the spirit realm will reward you *openly*. That means in the natural realm. This verse is teaching prosperity. God sees in the spirit realm, and you are an eternal being on the inside, in your spirit. When you decide in your inner man what you are going to do, God sees it and rewards it openly. That is where it comes back good measure, pressed down, shaken together and running over, shall *men* give into your bosom. (Luke 6:38.)

9

Be Effective in Prayer

MATTHEW 6:5

And when thou prayest, thou shalt not be as the hypocrites are: for they love to pray standing in the synagogues and in the corners of the streets, that they may be seen of men. Verily I say unto you, They have their reward.

In the last section, we learned that hypocrites always put on a mask, so that people will see something different than what they really are. Notice they love to pray "standing in the synagogues" and "in the corners of the streets." If you want maximum exposure, stand on the street corners; that's where the two roads cross. That's where they prayed. Jesus called them hypocrites because they were not doing it to God, they were doing it unto men.

Jesus said, "When men say 'Oooh and Ahh' and 'Isn't he deeply spiritual?' go ahead and soak it up; because that's the only reward you're going to get."

VERSE 6

But thou, when thou prayest, enter into thy closet, and when thou hast shut thy door, pray to thy Father which is in secret; and thy Father which seeth in secret shall reward thee openly.

He tells you two things to do in this verse. First is "enter into thy closet." *Closet* is an old English word which means "private bed chamber," your bedroom. Find a place where you can get private with the Lord. Second, shut the door.

When you go into your bedroom, you get away from the *world*; when you shut the door, you get away from the *family*. Shutting the door indicates that you're really going to get private — just you and God. No one else can see what is going on.

When you are in private He says to "pray to your Father which is in secret; and thy Father which seeth in secret shall reward thee openly." Again, the word "openly" here indicates there are even natural rewards for prayer. The prayer of faith can get you something now. It can get you healed; it can get finances for you; it can get you things that you need here in this life. So, prayer does bring about rewards that can be seen.

Praying can also bring about physical relaxation or a physical refreshing. You can't always take a vacation when you get tired, so what do you do? Begin to pray in the Spirit. (Is. 28:11,12.) There have been times when I got in my car and turned off the radio and as I was going down the road, I just prayed and prayed and sang in the Spirit and ministered to the Lord. The refreshing that I had in my spirit as I began to minister to the Lord just bubbled right over and went on into my body and refreshed my body, too. When I would get out of the car, I would be in better condition than when I got in. I took a ten minute vacation!

Be Brief and to the Point —

VERSES 7,8

But when ye pray, use not vain repetitions, as the heathen do: for they think that they shall be heard for their much speaking.

Be not ye therefore like unto them: for your Father knoweth what things ye have need of, before ye ask him.

These verses are talking about something very important: When you pray in faith, keep it short and to the point.

Your heavenly Father knows what you have need of, but the Word of God tells you to put Him in remembrance of His Word. (Is. 43:26.) To put God in remembrance of His Word, you have to *know* the Word first. ". . . faith cometh by hearing, and hearing by the Word of God (Rom. 10:17)." Therefore, to have faith, you must know the Word of God.

God's Model Prayer —

VERSE 9

After this manner therefore pray ye: Our Father which art in heaven, Hallowed be thy name.

Notice He doesn't say, "Pray this prayer." He says, "Pray after this manner." This prayer is called the Lord's Prayer but it really is not; it is a model prayer. As a model prayer, it is simply a scaffolding for prayer: You can hang prayers on it.

"Our Father." Immediately you're identifying Who your prayer is to: You're approaching God, not as God, but as Father. Too many religious people approach Him as God. His children know how to approach Him as Father when they pray in faith.

Beginning with the word "hallowed," in this verse, every sentence in the prayer is written as a command.

The first thing you're saying is, "God, Your name be sanctified and set apart." God is holy, the Bible says; He is the sanctifier.

VERSE 10

Thy kingdom come. Thy will be done in earth, as it is in heaven.

Some people jump on this verse immediately and say, "He is instructing His disciples to pray for the coming millennial kingdom."

That's not it at all. Yes, this has millennial applications to it, but this is not talking about the Millennium. The Jewish people thought the millennial kingdom was coming at any minute. That is why they thought Jesus came to earth. They knew that according to Old Testament prophecy, when the Messiah came, the millennial kingdom was right on His heels. So when Jesus was talking about the kingdom, they were thinking about the millennial kingdom. They didn't see the church age which is a preview of the Millennium which is to come.

The Dispensations —

There are seven main dispensations in the Word of God. The first dispensation was the Dispensation of *Innocence*, which began with the creation of Adam and ended with the Fall. The next dispensation was *Conscience*, which ended with the Flood. After the Flood came the Dispensation of *Human Government*, and it ended with the Tower of Babel. Next came the Age of *Promise*. This was the dispensation in which Abraham lived and it ended in Egypt.

After the Dispensation of Promise came the *Law*, or the Dispensation of the Jew. The Dispensation of the Law ended at the cross, but the Jewish Dispensation has never ended.

Next came the *church age* which is also called the Dispensation of Grace. The church age began with the outpouring of the Holy Spirit on the day of Pentecost and is called "the last days."

It says in Acts 2:17, "And it shall come to pass in the last days, saith God, I will pour out of my Spirit upon all flesh . . . ." The church age will go all the way until the Rapture, and after the Rapture, the earth will go into seven years of tribulation. When Jesus went to the cross, the Jewish time period stopped, but it never came to an end. There are still seven years of Jewish time left to be fulfilled. Those last seven years are the Tribulation.

After the Tribulation will come the last dispensation which is the *Millennium*. So, the seven dispensations are Innocence, Conscience, Human Government, Promise, Law, Church, and the Millennium.

Jesus gave this model prayer three years before He went to the cross. They were living in the Dispensation of the Law. There were two dispensations still to come — the church age and the Millennium. He taught for all dispensations. Jesus was setting down the platform for the kingdom.

This Is Your Millennium —

If you've accepted Jesus as your Savior, *your* millennium has come. The Holy Spirit brought the kingdom to the earth on the day of Pentecost and we entered into it. Since that day, we've been living in those last days.

In the Millennium, the physical body of Jesus will come down to this earth and rule and reign. Right now the Lord is doing through the Body of Christ, the church, what He will be doing in the Millennium worldwide.

"Oh, no, I don't believe we've entered our millennium because during the Millennium, there won't be any sickness," someone might say.

That's right.

"Yes, but during the Millennium there is going to be universal prosperity," they say.

That's right. We've entered our millennium.

"Yes, but during the Millennium, the knowledge of the Lord will cover the earth as the waters cover the sea."

That's right. We're living in the day of the outpouring of revelation knowledge. Some of you might be surprised when you come back in the Millennium, and it is no different than what you have right now. All this time, you've been waiting for it to come, and you've had it all the time — prosperity, health and other blessings.

"Yes, but during the Millennium, the devil will be bound," they say.

That's right. He's bound already, isn't he? Ephesians tells us that he's already under our feet. Colossians says that Jesus spoiled principalities and powers and made a show of them openly. You should have no more fear of the devil now than you will then — and you won't have any fear of him then because he'll be bound in the bottomless pit with chains. He's been going around *as* a roaring lion, but he's bound. Jesus bound him for me.

"Yes, but during the Millennium there won't be any physical death."

Well, I'll tell you one thing — we're probably in that generation that's going to miss physical death. We're going to get raptured. But if we do have physical death, Jesus took the sting out of it. Physical death is merely graduation day, and I'm going to leave this earth without sickness or disease. When I die, I'm just going to step over into glory.

I used to wonder why Peter quoted a millennial passage out of the book of Joel on the day of Pentecost. "But this is *that* which was spoken by the prophet Joel; And it shall come to pass in the last days, saith God, I will pour out my Spirit upon all flesh: and your sons and your daughters shall prophesy, and your young men shall see visions, and your old men shall dream dreams" (Acts 2:16,17). If you go back and study it, you'll see Joel was talking about when Jesus ushers in the Millennium and he calls it "the last days." Peter quoted that passage because he knew, "Hey folks, we've entered *our* millennium."

"Thy will be done in earth, as it is in heaven." Is there a devil in heaven? No.

Is there sickness or poverty in heaven? No.

Whatever you bind on earth is bound in heaven, and whatever you loose on earth is loosed in heaven. (Matt. 18:18.) Heaven and earth work together. As God works in heaven, man should be working on earth.

VERSE 11

Give us this day our daily bread.

This prayer is for someone who is mature in the Word and can remind God of His promises. This is not a petition; this is a command. Bread is a necessity of life, and the Bible says your needs are supplied according to His riches in glory by Christ Jesus. (Phil. 4:19.) The way you can command bread from God is to remind Him that He told you it is already yours.

Notice He's only asking for bread one day at a time. Men are always trying to hoard, store up and make plans for tomorrow. That's the lazy approach. If we could hoard up for a year, we wouldn't have to use our faith again for a whole year. We wouldn't have to believe God or study His Word. We could just sit back and do nothing. There is always a tendency on our part to want to do that, isn't there? But as long as our bread is provided a day at a time, we have to use our faith tomorrow like we did today, right?

VERSE 12

And forgive us our debts, as we forgive our debtors.

People sometimes think that verse means that God forgives you in the same way that you forgive other people. That's not true, because although we forgive each other, there is always a tendency to remember it later, and let it start to fester up again. That never will happen with God. Once He forgives you, He forgets it entirely.

This verse is saying that God cannot forgive us *until* we exercise forgiveness. If a brother and I have something against each other, God can't forgive me as long as I'm harboring something against him. I have to forgive him, and wipe that out and then God can forgive me. This verse is indicating that He will forgive us *as* we forgive others.

VERSE 13

And lead us not into temptation, but deliver us from evil: For thine is the kingdom, and the power and the glory for ever. Amen.

We can trust God not to lead us into temptation because He's already said in James 1:13 that He tempts no man with evil. The actual Greek translation of this says deliver us from "the evil one." The evil one is, of course, the devil. Has He delivered us from the evil one? Yes. So put Him in remembrance of it.

The second part of this verse is not found in many of the original manuscripts. But whether or not it is found, it's still true. His *is* the kingdom. His *is* the power, His *is* the glory forever.

VERSES 14,15

For if ye forgive men their trespasses, your heavenly Father will also forgive you:

But if ye forgive not men their trespasses, neither will your Father forgive your trespasses.

These verses amplify . . . "forgive us our debts, as we forgive our debtors." God forgives us as we maintain a forgiving heart and as we forgive those who wrong us.

Jesus gave us an excellent model prayer. It is a prayer of faith. But it is a prayer not everyone can pray. Only those who know the Word can put God in remembrance of it, can pray it.

10
Fasting Changes You

The third area of righteousness on which Jesus instructs His disciples in Matthew 6 is fasting. If there is anything that has been carried to an extreme today, it is fasting. There are books out on fasting; some even tell you that fasting is the answer to all your problems. They say if you want a girlfriend, fast and God will get you one. If you want a better marriage, it will make your marriage better. According to the books, everything revolves around fasting.

Remember, fasting, praying and giving are not done to move God. A lot of people think that you can change God through fasting. That would make God subject to you. God's blessings would be subject to our works. That's blasphemy. You cannot bribe God with fasting. You cannot fast and make God do anything. Neither can you give and make God do anything. God is unchangeable.

All these things — fasting, praying and giving — are to change *you*, not God. If you become more liberal in your giving, you change. If you become more effective in prayer, you change. If you fast, it will change you.

Fasting is not going without food; that is dieting, and that's not spiritual at all. Fasting is setting aside time that you normally would spend doing bona fide things such as eating, watching television, and other things and substituting for them prayer and study of the Word. It's not the doing without food that is important; it is getting into God's Word that is important.

For example, if every day from noon until 1 p.m. you go to lunch, that is a bona fide thing you do. No one would look at you and say, "Eating is wrong." No, eating is fine; we need to eat. One day you decide that instead of eating lunch you're going to study God's Word and pray. You are substituting the Word of God and prayer for eating: rearranging priorities.

Another example of fasting would be if you gave up watching the news. There is nothing wrong with the news. What if you did without the news every night for a week and you substituted for it the study of the Word of God and prayer? That would be three and one half hours more you would get in the Word that week.

MATTHEW 6:16

Moreover when ye fast, be not, as the hypocrites, of a sad countenance: for they disfigure their faces, that they may appear unto men to fast. Verily I say unto you, They have their reward.

The hypocrites in this verse are those who put on a big show with fasting. They change their countenance so men will know that they are fasting. They want men to see something different; they want to brag with their countenance. They disfigured their faces by rubbing ashes on them.

Many times in the Old Testament, people would repent in sackcloth and ashes, but they were doing it before God and not before men. But, these men put on ashes just so men would think they were spiritual. That is what makes it wrong. Fasting, praying and giving are all wrong if all you are looking for is the glory and the approbation of men. When all someone wants to do is give, pray and fast so that men will pat them on the back, that is called approbation lust. It's worse than dope because a little bit of it won't suffice. It has got to be done day after day. More pats on

92

the back demand more pats on the back. You have to break out of that mold by getting before God.

The only pat on the back I want is from God. If I seek after favor with God, then favor with men will come. If you're trying to please men, you're going to be so frayed after awhile because you can't please everyone. But, if you seek God, you've only got to do one thing — follow His Word. If every other man turns away from me, as long as God pats me on the back, that's fine.

VERSE 17

But thou, when thou fastest, anoint thine head,
and wash thy face.

To "anoint thine" head means to use perfumes or colognes. When you're fasting food you have to drink plenty of liquids. That causes your body to flush out poisons and you don't smell very good. Don't use that as a big facade before men to prove that you're fasting. Splash a little cologne or perfume on and wash yourself. Keep yourself clean.

VERSE 18

That thou appear not unto men to fast, but unto
thy Father which is in secret; and thy Father, which
seeth in secret, shall reward thee openly.

Is it wrong to tell people that you are fasting? No. There are times you have to. If you're in a road ministry, and you're staying at someone's house and you are fasting, before they start to make a big meal for you, tell them you are fasting. But also tell them not to spread it around. You're not fasting to be seen by men.

"And thy Father which seeth in secret," this is in the spirit realm, "shall reward thee openly," that is in the natural realm. There are natural rewards for fasting. The biggest reward is you can hear from God. When you hear from Him, you know what His will is. And knowing that can change your life!

11
Set Your Priorities

A lot of people would have listed money and earthly possessions back in Matthew 5 where Jesus talks about *sin*. Jesus talks about them in chapter 6 with all the *good* things — giving, praying, and fasting — because, in and of themselves, riches are not wrong, anymore than fasting, praying or giving. What is important is what your priorities are. If you're praying to be seen of men, you're wrong. If you want riches so men can see how great you are, you're wrong. If you are trying to have possessions to keep up with the neighbors, you're wrong.

MATTHEW 6:19

Lay not up for yourselves treasures upon earth, where moth and rust doth corrupt, and where thieves break through and steal.

People say, "Jesus is talking here against prosperity." He is not. He was saying, "Don't lay up treasures. Don't *hoard* them."

You could turn on the television any day and hear some religious leaders telling you to stockpile dried fruits and canned goods because hard times are coming. The way to get through hard times is not by *hoarding*, it's by *giving*. Hoarding is against the Word of God. There's a lot of teaching today which says the church or part of the church is going to go through the Tribulation. In fact, there is some teaching that there is no Rapture and that we're *all* going through the Tribulation; and therefore we need to hoard food. If there were no Rapture, and we were going through the Tribulation,

I wouldn't want to be the only one on the block with food. What if the news got out that I had some food? Don't hoard. Give it away, because as you give, it will come back to you on every wave. God will provide for you if you'll learn to be a giver.

"But what if hard times come?" someone might ask.

Then hard times will come but not on me.

"But what if there is no gas?"

I'll have it.

"But aren't you worried about tomorrow?"

No. If I have it today, I'll have it tomorrow because God is the same yesterday, today, and forever. (Heb. 13:8.) He's still the same; He never changes. If He supplied my needs yesterday and today, He'll provide my needs for tomorrow.

The first thing Jesus said is, "Don't hoard here on earth because moths can get through and corrupt it." Moths attack clothing. Don't hoard clothing.

Someone might say, "So, is it wrong to have nice clothing?"

No, just don't hoard it. The nice clothing you have from two and three years ago that you don't wear anymore, give to someone who has need of them.

The next thing He says is, "rust corrupts your treasure." Rust attacks metal objects like silver and gold. Don't hoard it. Some people think, *I'll put my clothes in a cedar closet or I'll keep the precious metal rubbed down. No moths or rust will get my treasure.*

Next He says, "Where *thieves* break through and steal." How will you stop that? "My angels will protect it," someone says. Not if you're *hoarding* they won't. They'll stand there with their arms folded and watch the thief go in and come back out with all your goods. You can't dismiss one part of the Word and think the rest of it will protect you. It won't work. You have to follow it *all*.

Where Is Your Heart —

VERSES 20,21

But lay up for yourselves treasures in heaven, where neither moth nor rust doth corrupt, and where thieves do not break through nor steal.

For where your treasure is, there will your heart be also.

Here "your heart" is referring to your thoughts. Wherever your treasure is, that is where your thoughts will be. If you're constantly hoarding money on earth, then every thought will be, *How can I get more?*

The Bible says, "Set your affection on things above, not on things on the earth. For ye are dead, and your life is hid with Christ in God" (Col. 3:2,3). The Greek word *affection* is literally *mind*. Set your *mind* on things above and not on things of the earth. Where your treasure is, there will your mind or thoughts be also. That introduces the next scripture.

VERSE 22

The light of the body is the eye: if therefore thine eye be single, thy whole body shall be full of light.

Natural light comes through the eye, but you don't see with the eyeball; it is just the window where the light comes in. You see in your brain. That's what He is saying. The brain is actually where you see, but the light comes into the body through the eyeball.

The eye here speaks of the *mind* or the thoughts. He is saying that it is best to be a single-minded person. Get your mind on the Lord, keep your purpose *single*.

VERSE 23

But if thine eye be evil, thy whole body shall be
full of darkness. If therefore the light that is in thee
be darkness, how great is that darkness!

An evil eye is being double-minded. This man is
"unstable in all his ways." (James 1:8.) If you are single-
minded or have singleness of purpose, your spirit man will
be full of light. But if you become double-minded, then your
body will be full of darkness. If you're full of darkness but
you think it's light, you've deceived yourself. How much
more deceived could you be?

VERSE 24

No man can serve *two* masters: for either he will
hate the one, and love the other; or else he will hold
to the one, and despise the other. Ye cannot serve
God and mammon.

Mammon is the Chaldean god of money. You cannot
serve God and money. In the Christian life, money is not
wrong. But, if you get your eyes on money, then you've lost
everything. Set your eyes on the Lord alone and money will
be there. If you'll serve the Lord, He'll make sure you always
have money.

Take No Thought —

VERSE 25

Therefore I say unto you, Take no thought for your
life, what ye shall eat, or what ye shall drink; nor
yet for your body, what ye shall put on. Is not the
life more than meat, and the body than raiment?

He is still talking about the material things of life. He
is not saying that you are never supposed to think about

your clothing. He is saying to take no thought (don't worry) where your clothing is coming from. I think about my clothes. Every morning I think about which ones I am going to put on, but I never open up the closet door saying, "Oh, I hope there are some clothes in there." I never go the the kitchen and open the refrigerator door saying, "I hope there is some food in here."

I never think about my clothing; God always supplies my clothing. The world is not my source: God is. And God is going to keep on supplying and supplying.

VERSE 26

Behold the fowls of the air: for they sow not, neither do they reap, nor gather into barns; yet your heavenly Father feedeth them. Are ye not much better than they?

Jesus and the disciples were sitting on a mountain when He gave them this sermon. There were birds all around them. Birds never think about tomorrow. They just always know their needs are going to be supplied for today.

By worrying about your food, Jesus says you just lowered yourself below the level of a bird. You're better than the birds, yet you're worrying about where your food is going to come from. Have you ever heard of a bird flying through the air saying, "I believe I receive; I believe I receive; I believe I receive"?

I'm not condemning those whose faith is on the line for food. I know many of you are believing God now for food on your table. But, God wants you to go beyond that. Get that behind you so that you can put your faith on bigger and better things than believing for every meal on the table. He wants you to get to the point where you never consider food anymore; to where you know that it is just going to be there, just like the birds do. Then take your faith and use it for healing, blessings, God's best for *others*.

If you always have to exercise your faith for food and clothing, the devil will keep you going in circles. You will never get anyone won to the Lord. Each morning you would get up, open the closet and say, "In the name of Jesus I believe there are going to be clothes in there." You would also open the cupboard and believe you would have food. I've been there. I have had to do that. But I left that level years ago. I don't even consider where food and clothing will come from anymore. I *always* have them. Sometimes the family has so much that we have to give some away.

VERSE 27

Which of you by taking thought can add one cubit unto his stature?

No matter what your need is, cast it off on the Lord. The Bible says to cast all your burdens and all of your anxieties off on the Lord because He cares for you. (1 Pet. 5:7.) Psalm 55:22 tells us, "Cast thy burden upon the Lord, and he shall sustain thee. . . ."

Jesus says everything should be cast off on the Lord. When you worry about it, you take it off the Lord and put it back on yourself. You're pushing God out of the way and saying, "Lord, I can handle this one." By wondering where it is going to come from, you're looking at yourself as the source. By putting it off on the Lord, God is the source and you don't have to worry about it.

When you take it off the Lord and start worrying about it, in your own estimation, you grew two inches because you said, "I can handle it." But you are the *only* one who thinks you have grown. Jesus said you haven't even added one cubit to your stature. What you have done is just lowered yourself; you fell below a bird!

Can you see where self-deception comes in? You think that you've gotten bigger, and God says that you have just fallen two notches — "O ye of *little* faith!" (Matt. 6:30).

And why take ye thought for raiment? Consider the lilies of the field, how they grow; they toil not, neither do they spin:

And yet I say unto you, That even Solomon in all his glory was not arrayed like one of these.

Wherefore, if God so clothe the grass of the field, which to day is, and to morrow is cast into the oven, shall he not much more clothe you, O ye of little faith?

Today lilies are a nice flower. Back in those days in Palestine they were as common as dandelions. They were everywhere. In fact, the disciples were probably sitting in the middle of a field of them. They were just a *common* flower: The more you tried to get rid of them, the more they kept coming back. He is saying here, "Through your own self-effort, you couldn't make yourself as good looking as a common flower. Even Solomon, arrayed in all his glory, didn't look as good as a lily.

He called lilies, "the grass of the field." They were as common as grass. In today's language we would say, "We mow the grass, bag it, put it out by the sidewalk for the trash man to pick up. A few days later, we mow it, bag it, and they come by and pick it up." Clothing is like grass: It will always be there and always keep multiplying, and you'll always have to keep pruning it and getting rid of it.

Do you get up in the morning and believe God that you're going to have grass in your front yard? No. You expect it to be there. Your clothing should be the same way. Always open your closet in the morning expecting to see clothes there. If you're always believing for your clothing and your food, your basic needs, then you are one of *little* faith. He does not say you are without faith, only that your faith is small.

VERSES 31,32

Therefore take no thought, saying, What shall we eat? or, What shall we drink? or, Wherewithal shall we be clothed?

(For after all these things do the Gentiles seek:) for your heavenly Father knoweth that ye have need of all these things."

The word *Gentile* is the same word as *heathen;* they both mean the same thing. The word *seek* means "to scrounge." So it could read, "After all these things are the heathen scrounging." The father of the heathen is the devil; no wonder they're scrounging. Your father is God. He owns the whole universe. Everything belongs to Him; so why are you out there scrounging like the heathen? You should be expecting your Father to supply.

My little boy comes into the kitchen and he knows food is going to be in there. He doesn't give it the slightest thought. He would be surprised if he opened up the refrigerator and there wasn't any food in there. My son would ask me, "Daddy, what is wrong?" I would have to come up with some pretty good answers. That ought to be our attitude. We should be shocked if we opened up the refrigerator and there was nothing there. But, you see, I'll never open the refrigerator and find it empty because God supplies for me; and I don't need to go out and scrounge and hoard. God supplies.

Set Your Priorities —

VERSE 33

But seek ye first the kingdom of God, and his righteousness; and all these things shall be added unto you.

This verse describes the single-minded man. He looks only to the Lord and His righteousness. Seeking first the

102

kingdom of God and His righteousness is seeking His Word. And *all* these things — food, drink, clothing, shelter and all the things of life — shall be added unto you.

VERSE 34

Take therefore no thought for the morrow: for the morrow shall take thought for the things of itself. Sufficient unto the day is the evil thereof.

The future is hidden from us and rightfully it should be. When you hoard and you put away, you're always trying to protect against the evil which might come tomorrow. Hoarding is motivated by fear. Don't fear the future; God is God of tomorrow as well as today. *Worry is always future.* Faith says, "God has provided my needs every moment until now," but worry says, "Ten minutes from now, it's all going to go under." Just live for today. When tomorrow comes, you'll have faith for tomorrow. When the next day comes, you'll have faith for it as well.

12
A Warning for
Mature Christians

As you set the priorities in your life — seek first the kingdom of God and His righteousness, you will seek God's Word and faith will come. When faith begins to come, you're going to please God. As you start pleasing God, you are growing and maturing. As you grow, you begin to set your affections on the Lord and not to think about the things of life. You know they are provided for you.

Matthew chapter 7 is a warning for the mature Christian. It's a warning against the sin of judging. Only mature Christians can judge because you have to have a little knowledge under your belt before you get puffed up. Suppose you start seeking the kingdom of God and His righteousness and these things are being added unto you. You're walking in prosperity and you begin to think, *I don't have to worry about anything; God has provided everything.* There is a tendency for you to get your nose up in the air just a little bit when someone else around you is having a little trouble. You think, *You poor peon. Why are you having trouble? Don't you know what I know? Faith is easy. You ought to just walk in faith.*

MATTHEW 7:1,2

Judge not, that ye be not judged.

For with what judgment ye judge, ye shall be judged: and with what measure ye mete, it shall be measured to you again.

The Gospel of Luke also gives an account of the Sermon on the Mount and includes something that Matthew left out.

Look at Luke 6:37,38, "Judge not, and ye shall not be judged: condemn not, and ye shall not be condemned: forgive, and ye shall be forgiven: Give, and it shall be given unto you; good measure, pressed down, and shaken together, and running over, shall men give into your bosom. For with the same measure that ye mete withal it shall be measured to you again."

Combining the two accounts, we read, "Judge not that ye be not judged. For with what judgment ye judge, ye shall be judged, and with what measure ye mete, it shall be measured to you again. Give and it shall be given unto you, good measure, pressed down, shaken together, and running over shall men give unto your bosom." This brings out both the negative and the positive of sowing and reaping. Matthew centers in on the theme of judging. Luke brings out the aspect of giving and receiving.

When you put the verses together, they are saying that you are going to reap what you sow. If you sow judgement, you'll reap judgement. If you sow love, you'll reap love. If you sow finances, you'll reap finances. Everything that you sow will always be brought back; but you'll reap much more than you sow. ". . . good measure, pressed down, and shaken together, and running over." How much is that? Let's find out.

VERSES 3,4

And why beholdest thou the mote that is in thy brother's eye, but considerest not the beam that is in thine own eye?

Or how wilt thou say to thy brother, Let me pull out the mote out of thine eye; and, behold, a beam is in thine own eye?

A mote is a splinter. Your brother has a splinter in his eye. But when you judge him, you get a beam (a log, a telephone pole) in your eye.

Throughout the entire Sermon on the Mount the eye has stood for the mind. (Matt. 5:29; 6:22,23.) Here we learn something very interesting: sin is soulish. You do not sin in your spirit. You sin in your *mind*, your soul. If your brother has judged you, done you wrong, or gossiped about you, he's got a sin in his soul. Now don't judge his splinter or you will reap a log.

Let me give you an example. Suppose someone is sitting in my meeting and doesn't agree with the teaching. He gets upset, walks out the door, and starts gossiping about me. "Did you hear what Bob said? I don't agree with that at all. In fact, I think Bob is way off." As he walks down the hall, someone hears him and tells me everything he said. I say, "Well, who does he think he is? After all, *I'm* the teacher. I'm God's man of faith and power; who does he think he is? That little peon doesn't know enough Word to fill a thimble."

What he did by gossiping about me was a *splinter* in his eye. But when I judged him, I reaped the splinter good measure, pressed down, shaken together and running over; I got a *log* in my eye.

Which one is worse — him gossiping about me, or me judging him? Judging is worse. I have enough Word in me so I should have known better, but I did it anyway. You get so puffed up with pride that the devil urges you on — "That's right. Go on, keep it up." *He* sees you with the log in your eye, but you don't even know it.

VERSE 5

Thou hypocrite, first cast out the beam out of thine own eye; and then shalt thou see clearly to cast out the mote out of thy brother's eye.

There are two extremes in teaching on this subject. One extreme says, "Don't judge this man." The other extreme says, "If he's got a problem, leave him alone, because you might get into judging him by helping him." Both are wrong. I don't want to judge him, but I don't want to go to the other extreme and leave him alone. The Word says if your brother is in need, you ought to help him. (Gal. 6:1.)

When my brother starts to gossip about me, and someone comes and tells me, it is up to me, out of concern and compassion, to go to him and help him get that splinter out of his eye *without* creating a log in my own eye.

When my little boy comes in with a splinter in his foot, we don't amputate his foot to get rid of the splinter. But when most people hear about someone doing something wrong to them, they would just as soon yank the person's whole eye out just to get rid of the splinter. You can pull a thorn out of a foot with as little pain as possible. The same thing is true here. We get rid of the splinter without hurting the brother.

The Bible does say that you are to judge, but it doesn't say to judge people. It says that the spiritual man judges all *things*. (1 Cor. 2:15.) You can judge *things* without judging *people*. It is all right to judge the sin the person has committed, but don't hurt him; love him. In the meantime, try to get rid of the impurity without harming him.

Extracting the Splinter —

How are we supposed to pull the splinter out of the person's eye? Galatians 6:1 tells us. *"Brethren, if a man be overtaken in a fault, ye which are spiritual, restore such an one in the spirit of meekness; considering thyself, lest thou also be tempted."*

Notice who is supposed to help pull the splinter out of the eye — the one who is *mature* or *spiritual*. Remember what Paul said in 1 Corinthians 3:1. "And I, brethren, could not speak unto you as unto spiritual, but as unto carnal, even as unto babes in Christ." Only those in *fellowship*, without logs in their eyes are spiritual. They are the *only* ones who can help someone else. When you are helping someone, make sure you don't get puffed up in pride. The moment you do, you get a log in your own eye.

The word "restore" in Galatians 6:1 is a medical term, and it means "to reset a dislocated bone," not a *broken* bone but a *dislocated* bone. We never get broken because we are bones in the body of Christ and the Bible says, "He keepeth all his bones: not one of them is broken" (Ps. 34:20).

When we get out of fellowship with the Lord, we don't get broken; we get dislocated, and that's when we need spiritual believers to rally around us and help us get back into place. Dislocated bones are painful. In the body of Christ, when someone gets dislocated, everyone senses the pain. First Corinthians 12:26 says that when one member suffers, everyone suffers with it. When one member rejoices, everyone rejoices with it.

We are to restore such a one "in the spirit of meekness." Remain teachable. (Matt. 5:5.) You can profit from another person's mistakes. You can learn something while you're helping him. You can learn how he got into that situation and how you can steer clear of it yourself.

There have been times when I have counseled people and when they left, I had learned as much, if not more, than they had. I benefited from their mistakes. If I keep a teachable spirit while I'm resetting the dislocated bone, I can get an education myself.

When He says, *"Considering* thyself lest thou also be tempted," he means "to keep on examining yourself." While you are resetting the dislocated bone and helping your brother get back into fellowship with the Lord, you should constantly keep examining yourself, lest you also be tempted. To do what? Get puffed up with pride. There is a tendency while you're helping someone else to feel like you are a big shot — to get the attitude of a big brother helping the weak one. If you get that attitude, you will fall under a log. You will be judging them.

The attitude you need to keep is found in Galatians 6:2,3. *"Bear ye one another's burdens, and so fulfill the law of Christ."* The law of Christ is, "Thou shalt love thy neighbour as thyself" (Mark 12:31). *"For if a man think himself to be something, when he is nothing, he deceiveth himself"* (Gal. 6:3). Don't keep a big shot attitude while you're helping him. Just keep remembering that you have pulled a few boneheaded moves yourself. You have been in the same place he is and someone was sent to pick you up and help you. You're just doing the same for him.

"But let every man prove his own work, and then shall he have rejoicing in himself alone, and not in another"(Gal. 6:4). You stand alone before God. After you help a brother get back into fellowship and he has gone on his way, you're totally on your own, it's just God and you. All you stand accountable for is yourself. What that man does now is between him and God. You helped him get back to the position where he can help himself. After he's gone, don't say, "Boy, I bet God thinks I'm super; look at how I helped that guy." Don't rejoice in him.

Galatians 6:5 goes on to say, *"For every man shall bear his own burden."* Verse 2 said, "Bear ye one another's burdens." These two verses sound contradictory in the King James Version. The Greek word for "burdens" in verse 2 is *baros* which means "an extremely heavy weight." The Greek word for "burden" in verse 5 is *phortion*, a light burden. *Phortion* is the word found in Matthew 11:28-30 when Jesus said, "Come unto me, all ye that labour and are heavy laden, and I will give you rest. Take my yoke upon you . . . for

110

my yoke is easy, and my burden (*phortion*) is light." The burden Jesus gives you in life is light. The ministry is a burden because there are hardships in it, but the rewards are so great. You don't even notice it after awhile.

The Lord handed you a burden: He put it in your hand and you began to carry it. It's like carrying a lightweight ink pen. There is not a lot of weight to it; it's pretty easy to carry. That's a *phortion*. But, what if you have arthritis? That lightweight pen would suddenly turn into a heavy burden, *baros*. In fact, what you could normally pick up, suddenly becomes difficult to pick up.

God wants each person to be self-sufficient and carry his own burden (*phortion*). But when you get out of fellowship with the Lord, spiritual arthritis sets in. That arthritis causes that *phortion* to become a *baros*. It gets so heavy you need others to come around and help you lift it up until you again have strength enough in yourself to begin to carry it. Then your friends can go their way.

13
Walking in Maturity

In the first part of Matthew, chapter 7, Jesus is talking to believers about being mature. In verses 1-5, He speaks of carnal believers — ones who get out of fellowship with God by judging others. We see that getting out of fellowship is not just something that happens to babies; mature Christians get out of fellowship, also. In verses 6-12, He talks about spiritual believers.

Protect Your Pearls —

MATTHEW 7:6

Give not that which is holy unto the dogs, neither cast ye your pearls before swine, lest they trample them under their feet, and turn again and rend you.

In the Bible, pigs and dogs are both types of unbelievers. Pigs are types of Jewish unbelievers, and dogs are types of Gentile unbelievers. "That which is holy" and "pearls" refer to nuggets from the Word of God — things that are revealed to you.

When you're studying God's Word and God reveals something to you, there is a tendency to get so excited that you run out the door, grab the first person you find and share your revelation. Many times that is dangerous for both believers and unbelievers.

Never share anything like that with unbelievers. There's only one thing you tell unbelievers and that's the message of salvation, period. There is a tendency sometimes to want to tell them all about the endtimes, the common market nations, the mark of the beast, the international monetary system and the anti-Christ. They might look at you and say, "Boy, that's really neat; where did you learn that?" But so what? If they walk away unsaved, what good is it?

With unbelievers the whole issue is salvation: believe on the Lord Jesus Christ. Keep it simple.

God doesn't give you revelations for nothing. There will be times you will need that revelation and you'll be able to preach it or share it, but wait for the right time.

When I get a revelation from the Word and run out and share it with another Christian, one of two extremes usually occurs. I see that the subject is either too far over their head and they don't understand it at all, or I share it with someone who learned it ten years before. He looks at me and says, "Oh, are you just *now* finding that out?" All the wind goes out of my sails.

I remember one day as I was studying in the Word and the Lord showed me something in a verse and I wanted to run out and share it. But, I just sat on it for a little while. A few days later, someone came to me with a problem. The answer to their problem was exactly what the Lord had shown me. I had the revelation for them! I waited for the right moment. God knows what is coming in the future, and if you'll hold onto your revelation in prayer, He will open the door for you to share it.

Ask, Seek, Knock —

VERSES 7-11

Ask, and it shall be given you; seek, and ye shall find; knock, and it shall be opened unto you:

For every one that asketh receiveth; and he that seeketh findeth; and to him that knocketh it shall be opened.

114

Or what man is there of you, whom if his son ask bread, will he give him a stone?

Or if he ask a fish, will he give him a serpent?

If ye then, being evil, know how to give good gifts unto your children, how much more shall your Father which is in heaven give good things to them that ask him?

These verses are talking about coming before the Lord, and always being assured that you will receive from Him what you asked.

Notice that *ask*, *seek*, and *knock* come in chapter 7 which talks about maturity. YOU cannot properly ask the Lord until you reach maturity. You can ask the Lord for things when you're young in the Lord, but most of the time, the way you ask it, and the things you are asking for, usually are not in line with God's will. God does not answer every prayer; He answers the prayer of faith. The only way you can have faith is by hearing, and hearing by the Word of God. This means you have to know the Word of God to properly apply prayer.

When you pray properly, He says that whatever you ask for, you're going to receive. You won't ask God for something good, and Him give you something that will harm you.

The three steps — ask, seek, knock — actually show a growing process. Is there a difference between asking and knocking? Yes, asking is more like, "Lord, please. I petition You. Would You do something for me?" Knocking gets into more demanding, like saying, "In Jesus' name, I believe I receive." But what is it that comes between asking and knocking, being bashful and being bold. It is *seeking* God's Word.

Stop and think about some of the prayers that you prayed when you first got born again. They were full of, "Lord, please, if it be Your will." There was more fear in approaching the throne of God than anything else. You were afraid that maybe He wouldn't answer or maybe He was too busy for you.

In the meantime, you started seeking God's Word and found out what your rights and privileges are, and your asking turned into knocking.

Now you walk right up to the door of God and say, "It's Your son, Lord, open up." He opens up. You say, "I need this, and I have need of that, and Your Word says this." You put Him in remembrance of His Word, then you close the prayer in the name of Jesus, thank Him that it is done according to Mark 11:23 and 24; you walk away assured that the answer is yours. That's the kind of prayer God likes.

But, again, there's a growing process of asking, seeking and knocking. Is it God's will that you ask Him? Of course. But, He wants you to move into the perfect will of God where you know your rights and privileges in the Word.

Some people teach that God won't give you everything you ask for, but whatever He gives you is the best thing for you. I read a poem one time that said, "I asked for riches, and I got poverty so that I may have need of Him. I asked for health, and He gave me sickness so that I could further depend on Him." It implied that if you got well, you would forget about God. That's junk. My children don't need to be sick to depend on me. Churches taught that for years because they were living off experience and emotion. But there's a new generation that's seeking God's Word. They do not come in fear to ask of God. They *knock* on the door and say, "Your Word says . . . ." That's boldness in God's presence.

Do Unto Others —

VERSE 12

Therefore all things whatsoever ye would that men should do to you, do ye even so to them: for this is the law and the prophets.

This verse is often called the Golden Rule: "Do unto others as you would have them do unto you." This is one verse of scripture that fulfills all the law and the prophets; "Love thy neighbour as thyself" (Lev. 19:18). The Golden Rule is no more than Leviticus 19:18. Do unto them as you would have them to do unto you. Sow seeds into a person so that they will treat you as you want them to treat you. If you want a person to love you, sow seeds of love into them. On this, the Word says, hangs all the law and the prophets. (Matt. 22:40.) James 2:8 calls this "the *royal* law."

14
Warning for the Multitudes

In the beginning of the Sermon on the Mount, Jesus was teaching His disciples only. As He gets to the end of it, the multitudes again find Him. They are again starting to gather around Jesus. In verse 13, the Sermon on the Mount makes an abrupt change. Jesus quits talking about maturity and asking the Father for things. Suddenly, He starts talking about salvation, entering the narrow gate, going down the narrow path, and about being cautious of false prophets.

Jesus begins to direct His attention away from the disciples and to the multitudes that are gathered around Him. He issues warnings to the whole crowd instead of just the disciples.

Gateway to Heaven —

MATTHEW 7:13,14

Enter ye in at the strait gate: for wide is the gate, and broad is the way, that leadeth to destruction, and many there be which go in thereat:

Because strait is the gate, and narrow is the way, which leadeth unto life, and few there be that find it.

This is a basic salvation message. Jesus says here, "Enter ye in at the *strait* gate." It should say the *narrow* gate. In the *King James Version* two words — strait and narrow — have been sadly interchanged. According to other translations, it should say the *narrow gate* and the *straight way.*

So it should read, "Enter ye in at the *narrow* gate: for wide is the gate, and broad is the way that leadeth to destruction, and many there be which go in thereat. Because *narrow* is the gate and *strait* is the way, which leadeth unto life and few there be that find it."

This verse is talking to unbelievers. Why does He compare Christianity, or coming to Jesus, to the narrow gate? Because there is only *one* way to eternal life, and that's through the Lord Jesus Christ.

A friend of mine was witnessing to a highly educated woman one day at a bus station. He started talking about Jesus, and she mentioned all the other religious leaders around the world. He would start talking about Jesus, and she would mention Mohammed. He would talk about Jesus, and she would bring up Buddah. Each time he started to quote the Bible, she would bring up something that some other religious leader said that was close to the same thing. Then he said, "Wait a minute; let's get back to Jesus. What do you think about Jesus?"

She said, "I think He was very broad-minded."

He said, "I don't. I think He was very narrow-minded. He said, 'I am *the* way, *the* truth, and *the* life: no man cometh unto the Father, but by *me*.' That's about as narrow-minded as you can get."

That is what Jesus was saying in this verse, "*I* am the door. I am the *only* door. It's a very narrow door, because I'm the only way to eternal life."

You could take all the other religions, all the brotherhoods, all the do-good systems and line them up side by side and they would all fit through the wide door that leads to destruction. If you want to find the way to eternal life, there's only one way, and that's through the Lord Jesus Christ. That's the narrow gate.

You and I happen to be living in a privileged dispensation in which the Holy Spirit is being poured out around the world, and we're seeing people swept into the kingdom day by day. There has never been a time like this time. There has never before been a time that you could turn on the television any day of the week and see the gospel being taught. Every day you turn on the radio and more and more stations are broadcasting the gospel. The Lord is coming soon, and the Holy Spirit is being poured out. But if you look at Christianity during the past 2000 years, you'll see that what Jesus is saying here is exactly true: "few there be that found it." Few found eternal life.

Although we're having people getting born again by the masses today, this statement is still true. Overall, it's a small number that are finding their way to eternal life compared to the masses entering hell each day.

False Teachers —

VERSE 15

Beware of false prophets, which come to you in sheep's clothing, but inwardly they are ravening wolves.

False prophets are religious teachers. Through the whole Sermon on the Mount, we have seen that they are different on the inside than they are on the outside. They are hypocrites. Jesus says that religious leaders or false prophets are ravening wolves on the inside but on the outside, they put on sheep's clothing. They are putting on a facade. Jesus called them whitewashed tombstones: on the outside they are pretty and white, but on the inside they are full of dead men's bones. (Matt. 23:27.) Religion always has a form of godliness on the outside, but it has no power on the inside.

When Christians are out of fellowship with the Lord, they also put on a facade. They walk around trying to make everyone think they are all right, but they are in the same boat as the unbeliever.

The Lord impressed something upon me as I was teaching this one day. He said to me, "False prophets come in *sheep's* clothes, not in *shepherd's* clothes." He said that they infiltrate the *congregation;* they don't try to take over the *pulpit.* They try to split the congregation. They try to come in as one of the sheep. Wolves don't want to eat the shepherd; wolves want to eat the sheep. They disguise themselves as sheep and infiltrate the congregation.

Do you know who they manage to sweep off their feet and take away? The babies — those who haven't been born again very long. They steal the babies or pervert the teaching and take them off in error.

VERSE 16

Ye shall know them by their fruits. Do men gather grapes of thorns, or figs of thistles?

It's interesting what He doesn't say. He doesn't say, "You'll know them by their *teaching,*" because a lot of the time their teaching *sounds* good; but it isn't. False teachers never come in with the poison first; they always bring meat first, and they mix poison with it. If you're going to poison a dog, you don't throw a slab of poison in front of him, because he won't eat it. You mix it with a good steak; he'll eat it and die.

That is the way false teachers are. Their doctrine is close to the truth. They say many things that are right. Then, on the heels of it, they stick in error. When all the babies are sitting around, the false teacher starts teaching things that are good and right. As all the babies are saying, "Yes, they teach the truth," the false teachers put in error, and the babies swallow it.

Check the Fruit —

How will you know false teachers? By their *fruit*. You may not agree with everything every teacher teaches, but if you look at the fruit they produce — the people they've seen saved and the lives they have touched — you'll know their ministry is in line with the Lord. If you see a person in the pulpit who seemingly is preaching the truth, yet he doesn't have any fruit in his ministry, there is something wrong.

VERSES 17, 18

Even so every good tree bringeth forth good fruit; but a corrupt tree bringeth forth evil fruit.

A good tree cannot bring forth evil fruit neither can a corrupt tree bring forth good fruit.

A good tree cannot *habitually* bring forth evil fruit. Once in a while, a tree will bring forth a bad fruit. You are a good tree, but that doesn't mean that every fruit you produce is going to be perfect because you might produce a sour grape now and then. You might have an orange that comes out a little brown rather than orange. Not everything you are going to do is going to turn out 100 percent accurate, but you don't habitually bring forth evil fruit.

VERSES 19, 20

Every tree that bringeth not forth good fruit is hewn down and cast into the fire.

Wherefore by their fruits ye shall know them.

When judgement time comes around, Jesus will look at our fruit. Aren't you glad He isn't going to judge us by our teaching? Aren't you glad He's going to overlook the times when we missed it? He is going to judge us on our production, our fruit. Those who habitually brought forth evil fruit out of their evil nature are going to be hewn down and cast into the fire.

There is another thing you can see here. Don't let it bother you because there are false teachers around. Leave them in the hands of the Lord. When it is all said and done, He's the one who is going to take care of all the trees — good and bad.

Do you remember the parable of the wheat and tares in Matthew 13:24-30? A man sowed good seed in his field. His enemy came while he slept and sowed tares among the wheat. When the wheat grew up, the tares appeared. The servants asked if they should pull out all the tares that had grown in with the good wheat. The householder said, "No, just wait until the reaper comes through and gets it all; it will all be handled at the time of the harvest." When the harvest is all brought in, Jesus is going to separate the wheat from the tares.

VERSES 21-23

Not every one that saith unto me, Lord, Lord, shall enter into the kingdom of heaven; but he that doeth the will of my Father which is in heaven.

Many will say to me in that day, Lord, Lord, have we not prophesied in thy name? and in thy name have cast out devils? and in thy name done many wonderful works?

And then will I profess unto them, I never knew you: depart from me, ye that work iniquity.

Here is an evil tree trying to say, "Yes, but Lord . . . ." The Lord is going to say, "There is no production, there is no fruit."

Immediately the question arises, "Yes, but how could they call Him Lord, and how could they say, 'We've done this in thy name?' " There are a lot of people talking *about*

124

Jesus today who don't know Him. Sinners are copying believers like never before. They are even using our terminology such as "born again," and most of them don't even know what being born again is.

Those who accept Jesus as their Lord and Savior, who do His will, are the ones who will enter into the kingdom of God. There's coming a day when He'll say to those wolves in sheep's clothing, "I never knew you: depart from me, ye that work iniquity."

15
Build a House That Will Stand

Jesus concludes the Sermon on the Mount with a practical application of the day's teaching. He invites all those who *heard* the sermon to *do* it, to *apply* what they *learned*, to make *knowledge* into *wisdom*. They too can be called "great" in the kingdom of heaven. (Matt. 5:19.)

Just because you're born again doesn't mean that you're immune to tests and trials, the winds and the waters. They are going to come, but your house can be established on the rock of the Word of God.

MATTHEW 7:24,25

Therefore whosoever heareth these sayings of mine, and doeth them, I will liken him unto a wise man, which built his house upon a rock:

And the rain descended, and the floods came, and the winds blew, and beat upon that house; and it fell not: for it was founded upon a rock.

The Wise Man —

The wise man built his house upon a rock, and the rain descended and the floods came. The rains and floods are types of persecutions of the devil. We face them every day. He never said we'll get away from persecution. We need to establish our house firmly so that it will *withstand* the persecution. Each of us faces persecution. But the stronger the foundation is, the better we'll endure it. When the floods come, the waters begin to rise, the winds blow and the waves start to beat against the house. You must be mature to handle the waves and the wind.

Ephesians 4:13 says to be mature. *"Till we all come in the unity of the faith, and of the knowledge of the Son of God, unto a perfect man* ('perfect' here means 'mature'), *unto the measure of the stature of the fulness of Christ."* Verse 14 goes on to say, don't be immature. *"That we henceforth be no more children, tossed to and fro* (this is referring to a ship being tossed by waves), *and carried about with every wind of doctrine. . . ."* The wind is compared to false doctrines. Who puts out false doctrines? False teachers — those who wear sheep's clothing and underneath, they are ravening wolves.

The waves are persecutions of the devil, and the winds are false doctrines of men. So, who is out there against you? The devil with circumstances of life and men with false teaching. You will come against them both and learn to withstand them.

What came against the house in Matthew 7:25? The flood water (the devil) and the winds (false doctrines of men).

It goes on to say in Ephesians 4:14, *". . . with every wind of doctrine, by the sleight of men, and cunning craftiness, whereby they lie in wait to deceive."* The words "sleight of men" in the Greek language are one word — *Kubia*. It is the root word for our English word *cube. Kubia* is the Greek word for *dice*. When you're immature, and you're *pushed* around by the devil, and blown *around* by the winds of false doctrine, you are in a crap game with the devil. The dice are loaded against you. There is no way you can win.

You say, "How do we know the dice are loaded?" Because it goes on to say *"in cunning craftiness."* That simply means *cheating*. The devil never plays fair. He always cheats.

Do you know what the devil does? He entices you by letting you win a little, then he socks it to you and drains every cent you have.

If you have ever gambled, you know that a dealer likes to feed you just a little bit, just to get you interested and excited and draw you in. He then takes you for all he can get.

When I went to Las Vegas to minister, a pastor said that he had met a boy on the street one day who was standing against a pole crying. The pastor went up to him and said, "What's wrong? I'm a pastor, and I know the Lord Jesus Christ; can I help you?"

The boy said, "I came here from New York just to have a good time, and I decided to gamble while I was here. I lost every cent I had. I live in New York, and I've got to be back to work. I don't have a penny to get home."

The gamblers didn't care; they didn't say, "We'll leave you enough to get home." They took it *all*. That's what the devil does. He robs you, strips you, takes all your clothes away, your billfold, your credit cards, everything, and you don't have anything left. Don't get caught in the devil's games.

You cannot win by getting on the devil's turf. The only way to win is to get the devil on your turf. You don't have to bow to him; he bows to you. The only way he's going to bow to you is for you to grow up and learn the Word. Build your house on the rock: Be a hearer and a doer of the Word.

Some people hear the Word but never do it.

VERSES 26,27

And every one that heareth these sayings of mine, and doeth them not, shall be likened unto a foolish man, which built his house upon the sand:

And the rain descended, and the floods came, and the winds blew, and beat upon that house; and it fell: and great was the fall of it.

Often we think that this is talking about the person who never comes to church. He didn't say the person didn't hear. He *heard*, but he didn't *do*. No, this person came to church and sat right beside the doer of the Word. Both of them heard the same message, but one person was not a "doer" of the Word he heard. He is called "least" in the Kingdom. (Matt. 5:19.)

Of the disciples who heard the Sermon on the Mount, there was one who was not going to be a doer of the Word — Judas. All of them were listening, but Judas did not turn into a doer of the Word. Some of the other disciples who were sitting there, picked certain parts of what Jesus said and became doers of that, but they didn't want to hear the other parts, so they shrugged them *off*. You must be a hearer and a doer of *all* of God's Word. You can't pick your favorite parts and disregard other parts, because the devil will come along at your weakest point, and he'll hammer and hammer until he gets your house to fall.

The only thing you can build your life on is the unchangeableness of God's Word; anything else is sand. Sand might look good for the moment, but it won't endure. The Word of God never changes.

When I went to high school, they taught me things that they said were backed by scientific evidence. But I can pick up a high school book of today, and it will tear down many things I learned then. Why? Because, they learned new things which make previous facts inaccurate. Man's knowledge is like shifting sand; but the Bible never changes. It's the only rock you'll find to build your life on.

He Taught With Authority —

And it came to pass, when Jesus had ended these sayings, the people were astonished at his doctrine:

For he taught them as one having authority, and not as the scribes.

They were astonished at His doctrine. No one said a word. They had heard Jesus preach, they had seen Him perform miracles, but they had never heard Him teach. He taught with such authority — not as the scribes. They were never dogmatic; it was always "It could be this way, we're not sure." They might say, "I'm going to give you five viewpoints, and you take your choice."

When Jesus spoke, it was, "thus saith the Lord." It's God's Word, and it never changes.

We don't bend the Word to meet our needs, we bend ourselves to meet the Word. When we move, shape and fit ourselves around the Word of God, that is when our life comes into perspective.

Bob Yandian, Pastor of Grace Fellowship in Tulsa, Oklahoma, has an anointing and extensive teaching background that enables him to convey the uncompromised Word of God with an everyday practical clarity. Primarily, Bob ministers to students of the Word — fellow full-time ministers, congregational members, and Bible school students.

A graduate of Trinity Bible College, Bob studied under its director and founder, Charles Duncombe, a contemporary and companion of Smith Wigglesworth. Bob also studied Greek at Southwestern College in Oklahoma City.

In 1972 Bob began teaching regularly at Grace Fellowship where he was a founding member. In 1973 he began working for Kenneth Hagin Ministries as Tape Production Manager then, in 1977, for Rhema Bible Training Center as a teacher. Later he became Dean of Instructors. In 1980 he began pastoring Grace Fellowship.

Bob has taught and ministered throughout the United States and Canada, in South Africa, Guatemala, and the Philippines. He has spoken at numerous Full Gospel Businessmen's Fellowship International meetings; the Greater Pittsburgh Charismatic Conference; Bill Basansky's 1981, 1982, and 1983 jubilees; Salt Lake Institute of Religion (Mormon); and hosted the Local Church Seminar at Grace Fellowship.